WORKING
Mothers

Also by Carol Dix

The New Mother Syndrome (Unwin Paperbacks, 1987)
Pregnancy: Everything You Need to Know (Penguin, 1985)
Say I'm Sorry to Mother (Pan, 1978)
The Camargue (Gollancz, 1975)

WORKING
Mothers

You : Your Career : Your Child

CAROL DIX

UNWIN
PAPERBACKS

LONDON SYDNEY WELLINGTON

First published in paperback by Unwin Paperbacks, an imprint of Unwin Hyman Limited, in 1989.

Unwin Hyman Limited
15–17 Broadwick Street
London W1V 1FP

Allen & Unwin Australia Pty Ltd
8 Napier Street, North Sydney, NSW 2060, Australia

Allen & Unwin New Zealand Pty Ltd with the Port Nicholson Press
Compusales Building, 75 Ghuznee Street, Wellington, New Zealand

British Library Cataloguing in Publication Data

Dix, Carol, 1946-
    Working mothers: you, your career, your child.
1. Great Britain. Working mothers. – Practical information
I. Title
305.4'3'0941
ISBN 0-04-440325-9

Typeset in 11 on 12½ Sabon by Computape (Pickering) Ltd and printed in
Printed and bound in Great Britain by
Cox & Wyman Ltd, Reading

CONTENTS

PROLOGUE

They say that childcare is going to be the issue of the 1990s. Certainly, working mothers are destined to move out of the ranks of the minorities and into that of the majority. The coming decade is likely to be beset by a whole new type of problem as the shrinking labour pool creates a skills shortage – the baby boom years are long gone and we are going to see fewer and fewer school-leavers and graduates seeking employment.

Suddenly, the women no one was concerned about, those who had in the past left the workforce to have babies, are going to be much in demand. The optimists believe that employers will now, as never before, begin making an effort to be more flexible: encouraging women who have babies to stay on at work, and persuading those who have left to stay at home with young children to return.

It will be interesting to see just what does happen. Is someone, somewhere, going to jump into action so that women who aspire to 'have it all' won't also find themselves struggling to 'do it all'?

Who knows? Perhaps in the future there will be part-time work, without loss of status; planned career breaks with guaranteed ease of return at the same level; training and support for women who have left a career for more than a few months to re-enter, with salary and benefits as perks; tax credits for childcare. One simple encouragement for women who have been out of the market for many years would be to offer a tax deduction, plus help with childcare provision, if she returns to work, backed up by more well-planned, light, airy nurseries, with decently paid staff and realistic hours, and after-school programmes for young children.

Women must make use of this decade. The only time we were needed in the past – during the Second World War – as everyone knows, nurseries sprouted in villages and towns. Arguments about how necessary it was for mothers to stay home were suddenly forgotten.

This may be a golden opportunity for women to seek the form of working life, with motherhood, that best suits them and their children.

Carol Dix
London, September 1988

1 BRAVE NEW WORLD ... OR BRAVE NEW WOMAN?

Career mothers. Working mothers. Women who work. Women who are mothers. There have been endless arguments in the past decade about the definitions of this new way of life that so many of us find ourselves a part of; a flesh and blood life experiment taking place within our own families. The arguments no longer centre so much on whether mothers *should* work, but have shifted to focus on the degree of stress experienced by the woman, her child, or her family (depending on which side you take, the stress moves around quite equitably).

Surprisingly enough, the pundits have been quietened on the basic question of why and under what circumstances a mother may work by the sheer numbers who have returned to the workforce after long, short, or even no breaks following childbirth. Psychoanalytic theory (or guesswork) has finally been superseded by sheer necessity.

Let me lay my cards on the table at the outset, as the author of this book which has asked women to look into the thorny issue of 'you, your career, your child'. I have chosen women who deliberately and willingly continued their work lives, whether as a planned career or a patchwork of jobs, once they became mothers. The book focuses on women who felt they would not be happy, or the best mother, if they remained home full time with their children. It is about women who have dealt personally with the various conflicts and complex juggling acts involved.

In no way is the book intended to be an attack on those who have chosen instead to devote a certain number of years to full-time mothering. My argument is not over the rightness or wrongness of mothers working, no more than a book (let alone a magazine article) has ever been devoted to the rightness or wrongness of a man continuing working once he has become a father.

I began the research and work for this book on the premise that a career is important to women. Work makes up a vital part of our intellectual, social and economic life – which never again should be belittled. As we move into the 1990s, perhaps the majority of women are going to expect to continue in their careers once they become mothers. So, we are now left not with the theories, the jargon, the scarred battlefield of who is wreaking most harm upon whom; but with the inner feelings, emotions, fears, happiness and, yes, guilt of real women out there in the real world.

The questions I have addressed, feeling they were of most importance, ran along the following lines. Just how are women coping with their careers? Are their bosses understanding, tolerant, able to be patient or forgiving? Are women still meeting with solid walls of resistance only overcome through dogged, hard work? How have they been treated when pregnant? Has maternity leave been easy to take, with legislation now firmly rooted in Britain to protect a woman's rights? Have subtle (or not so subtle) obstacles been placed in their way ready to trip up the smart and well-organised pregnant executive?

How are women fitting into the competitive, everyone-out-for-him-or-herself jungle in the field of promotions? How many are happy to put their career on hold for the time being? Is part-time work a satisfactory alternative? Can a woman put a career behind her for a few years and then expect to pick it up with the same amount of steam again? How many have found the going quite straightforward and easy; have many been finding it tough?

Ultimately the results of my research have been positive, forward looking and helpful. For the most part, the women I met, interviewed, talked to, are not complaining about their lot, though there is bitterness in some of the stories. A tone of wry irony at the vagaries of the system, and at some of the inequities still confronted in the male-dominated work world, best describes their overall perspective on the issue.

There is much less of a tone of apology about women working these days. Few put up reasons such as their need for money, or a second income, to explain their continuing in a career after motherhood. Women have accepted they enjoy their work. They hope to succeed. They have learned from previous generations that taking a year, not to mention five, out of a work life to raise young children leads to poorly paid and probably uninteresting work. It also perpetuates a system whereby women have been economically unequal, powerless and dependent upon men.

THE WOMEN WHOSE STORIES MAKE UP THIS BOOK

The responses of over 150 women, either to my questionnaire (which is reprinted in the Appendix) or during a more personal interview either face to face or by phone, make up the basis of this book. The written replies were graceful, articulate and the respondents generous with their time. I do want to thank everyone who became involved in this project — even if their particular stories have not been used; they took on the project as something important and meaningful, just as I had envisaged.

The sample I have used makes no claim to sociological truths or proportionate representation of all working mothers in this nation, or of any other. It is merely a self-selected sample of those women who read my request for involvement through a network of women's organisations; or of whom I learned through various other methods of research. As a working journalist of many years I am used to tracking down people willing to pour out their personal life stories and ideas into my notebook or tape recorder.

I never fail to be duly impressed at the spirit with which women and (in other cases) men become involved. How they are willing to give of their time, and the degree of articulateness with which they discuss their lives and ideas. The women who participated have become the 'main characters' of the book. I am reminded of the old saying – that inside everyone is a novel waiting to come out. Some of the contributions to this book should have the gripping appeal of a fictional account, but it is very much within the bounds of non-fiction. The only trick I have borrowed from the narrative form is to give each and every one of my respondents a fictional name and job: a necessary cover so they could afford to be truthful and thereby far more interesting.

The personal interviews all too often took place after 9 p.m., or at weekends. As a working mother myself, trying to find time to talk personally to other working mothers posed quite a problem. I have my own children to care for at the end of the day, and through a large part of the evening. My respondents had to finish work, rush home, maybe cook, play with their children, put them to bed and then find time to talk to me. But, as we know, today's working mothers are a resourceful lot. And when they're determined, they find the time.

A PERSONAL STORY

I had recently returned from living and working in New York when I began the research for this book. There, I had given birth to our two daughters and continued working through-out their early childhoods – albeit from home – as a writer. By the time we moved back to London, my daughters had reached the ripe old ages of 8 and 9. I had graduated from full-time childcare to the concerns of school and what happens afterwards. ˙

My own story is not typical of the women in this book, because I have not held down an out-of-the-home, full-time career during my mothering years. For that matter, I hadn't before motherhood changed my life either. I have long been a freelance writer. But I'm also a highly ambitious, success-oriented, determined woman who takes her work very seriously. In my own life, questions of how to fit children in with my work life never seem to be out of my mind.

Several years before the birth of my first child I had been aware, while working on a liberal and supposedly women-supportive newspaper, that few women there had children. The really successful female colleagues tended to be childless, often single. But, being part of the new baby-boom bulge generation, there were many other women nearing their 30s along with me, wondering just what they were going to do.

Working an evening shift, I recall feeling quite sick inside to watch a young (similar age) male journalist packing up to go home – clutching a huge cuddly bear in his arms. The image stuck in my mind. It all seemed so easy for him. A quick phone call, 'Hi, darling, I'll be on the 7.40 p.m. train. Little Joey hasn't gone to bed yet, has he?' and this man was successfully fulfilling his life, seeing that both his career and emotional needs were met. He had a wife at home of course, probably, in those days, a woman with a PhD to her name, who gave it all up 'for her family'. The sight of that cuddly bear brought tears to my eyes that evening. I was grappling with a problem: how was I ever going to fit a family in so easily and continue in that line of work with its long and anti-social hours?

The short answer: I left that prestigious and well-paying secure ship for the dangerous, but more flexible, rough seas of the freelance writer's life. Within a few years I had started my own family and it was then I knew what had motivated my apparently rash move away from 'the firm' (doesn't the corporate world offer a sense of 'family' to many men?). I had given myself time to build up a nest, whereby I could work and be around for my children. But, never, I have to admit, have those rough seas turned calm. The doubts and insecurities remain.

The nagging questions: did I 'give up' on the working world because I was afraid, or could not handle it on male terms? Did I opt out – and in doing so fail to allow myself real achievement? Should I have striven to become editor of a leading newspaper (or some other such highly visible achievement) rather than express my ambitions in a more passive, typically female way (though it would still be rather nice to pull in megabucks from a bestselling book!).

Because I was home based when my children were small, most people who didn't know me well assumed my work was more or less a hobby. In the competitive, difficult world of the self-employed writer (especially true of America), I don't know how they arrived at such an assumption. But it all fits in with the 'nice' woman doing her macramé, or something gently creative – filling her time between children's naps and school hours.

The truth of the matter was that I was newly living in America, struggling (dare I say it) manfully through that very tough jungle; starting again after a writing career I'd carefully built up and nurtured in London; coping with babies and young children; juggling my own intellectual and spiritual needs at the same time; dealing with a huge dose of inadequacy and sense of failure when I had to meet the stiffly groomed and outwardly successful magazine and book editors in New York.

A couple of times I did go back into newspaper offices to take up temporary, but full-time, positions. Once out there, trying to locate my tree and rope to swing from in that particular stressful jungle, I really appreciated just what other women were coping with in pursuing out-of-the-home, full- or part-time careers.

Without good help, or an exceptionally supportive husband, I could see that women were walking on a tightrope with an incredible number of jungle branches ready to trip them for a heavy fall if just one little thing should go wrong. Yet they're out there, walking admirably on that rope, keeping their heads and their balance, often against the odds. This book is in tribute to their courage, daring and expertise. What man would ever put himself through such a daily course of survival?

Within a decade women have made enormous changes in their inner lives. My own generation is now moving into our 40s. Younger women are moving into a world where maybe they won't even have to deal with some of the confusions we've struggled with – though I'm not altogether sure it will ever be downright easy. A story told me by another free-lancer friend paints the picture. Her 10-year-old daughter was going through some problems in her own life. And, in the time-honoured tradition of girls versus their mothers, she began to take out her fears and insecurities on my friend.

The girl was acting out her anger on her mother, on some occasions very outspokenly – no doubt trying to sort out in her own mind just where she fitted between 'mother' and 'father', 'female' and 'male' in this world. In one storming tantrum she began attacking her mother: 'You're a failure. Don't tell me you "work". What money do you make? You don't even wear nice clothes like the ladies in Daddy's office. Nothing you do ever succeeds. Daddy's successful. He has a "real" job. When I grow up I'm going to work in an office like Daddy.'

Holding her breath to fight off the tears, my friend, who was a struggling ceramic artist trying to fit in demanding work hours while giving her children time, felt the body blows coming from her daughter with real pain.

She was attacking everything I believed in, stood for, had fought for all these years. There she was telling me to be a modern woman, and work 'in an office'. Later on, when the anger had died down, in both of us, I talked to her about the choices and decisions women have to make in their lives.

I reminded her she loves babies, and often says she wants a big family. What was she going to do with her children while she worked at her office? 'Leave them with someone else,' she answered proudly. And then she hesitated. And we were both able to laugh. You see, she has never liked any of the babysitters I found for her. 'It's not easy, is it?' I said gently. Though I would like to think future generations will find the decisions less complex. At least, in the new world today, they're not so afraid of admitting their desires and needs.

WHY WE DON'T WORRY ABOUT BEING 'NICE' ANY MORE

On the basis of my research, I have noticed a healthy spurning of the old order – the one lived out by our mothers' if not grandmothers' generations. Gone is any lip-service to the notion of it's not being 'nice' for women to combine their two roles. More importantly, gone is the feeling of its not being 'feminine' to earn your own money, be proud of your work, to pursue an aggressively ambitious, or even non-aggressive but persistent, career path.

For all the arguments of the past decades on women's role, equal pay, liberation and independence, I feel now that the most positive direction is to be found in women's changing attitude to their careers.

Today's women no longer accept a traditional 'woman's place'. Some may be teachers, social workers, nurses or secretaries but for the most part they have entered lines of work comparable to their male equals. They have often been very successful. And they are determined to remain so, even if some choose to slow down while their children are young.

In the long run, women do have a certain advantage over men. By juggling work and motherhood, they are able to keep a perspective on life. They know that work is important, fun, rewarding, challenging, difficult, hateful, etc. But it's not everything. At the end of the day, if there is a child at home waiting to climb on her lap, that need will supersede any pressing business matter.

Balance and quality of life were terms that sprang to many lips during hours of conversation. Women are concerned that they do not merely emulate men, but that they try to keep control of these two important aspects of their lives.

CAN WE PLAN MOTHERHOOD TO FIT IN WITH A CAREER?

The young women, married or not, still childless, whom I met in the course of my research, talk earnestly about how they will fit motherhood in with their career plans. They worry how and when they will find the right time. Some break is obviously needed – but when? I hope this book will be of help to them in coming to some of those decisions. There are strategies women can devise – though as we all know the best laid plans can fall to pieces when human emotions and biology are taken into account.

WHO PAYS FOR CHILDCARE?

There is neither time nor space here to enter the discussion whether governments should be more involved in providing nursery care for working mothers. There are some excellent books that deal in depth with this most pressing issue. Sylvia Ann Hewlett's book, *A Lesser Life*, I found to be one of the most riveting reads as she delineated how not only men, but also radical feminists, have pushed the child-care issue to the back – stranding women ultimately with their own Catch 22.

You have to earn enough to ensure you can pay for adequate childcare before even beginning to think about actively pursuing a career. 'Modern superwomen are meant to have children on the side, "in their own time", and the less said about the matter, the better,' she writes. She also quotes a female executive, sitting on Ms Hewlett's own Family Policy panel, who refused even to talk about childcare provision: 'If a woman chooses to have children, then she should deal with the consequences,' were the executive's views.

Most of the women whose stories appear here indeed made their own childcare arrangements. They rarely even argued that the men in their lives should take a greater role in organising childcare. In the Resources section, I give some information on the current state of play in the governmental provision of workplace nurseries. But don't hold out much hope. It's a very short section! For the most part, the women here are typical in that they have accepted it's their role to pay a nanny, or a childminder – to find the full-time substitute for their 'maternal' care – so they can continue with their working lives unencumbered. Like a man.

These professional and determined women have taken on board the, as it were, God-given rule – if you're going to be out in the workplace, seriously, then it's up to you, the mother, to show us all that you're fulfilling that female part of your biological make-up – by arranging and orchestrating the substitute care of the child.

And, by and large, it is the women who are paying for the childcare. The money has to be found from their pay cheques. They arrange the hours and interview the potential employees. This is not – we have learned to understand – a role men are prepared to take on, never mind how nearly they resemble the 'new man' in other ways.

I'm sure there's room for change on that score. But I know from my own life that this is one area over which women have to retain control. If you are dependent on someone else to arrange that substitute care – the single most important part of the smooth running of your day – then you're potentially letting yourself in for trouble.

Who knows better than the mother herself what her children need; what sort of nanny or childminder they will like? Who else has her ear to the ground, her senses finely tuned to pick up on problems from child or childcare-substitute?

On these occasions, women *en masse* do seem to have given up the battle with men, or with male-dominated governments (in our case female-dominated but completely in line with macho ideals). They have acquiesced to the one intractable unwritten rule: 'If you're not going to be around to offer 24-hour mothering care, then it's up to you to arrange who will be.'

We'll have to leave this one to the next generation. For the time being, today's women seem intent to get on with their working lives and with enjoying their families. There is scant energy around for anything else. And certainly little to be left over for such major ongoing arguments.

WHAT SORT OF 'PRICE' DO WE PAY?

The message seems to be coming out quite clearly: women can combine motherhood and career very successfully. They will suffer an element of exhaustion. They may not achieve all the promotions they would have done without children. But they are prepared to accept such limitations because they want to fulfil both roles. The compromises are bearable.

WITHOUT GUILT ... WOMEN MIGHT BECOME JUST LIKE MEN!

Women today don't seem to feel they are compromising their mothering, though guilt just comes with the package that is motherhood. No doubt it has been proved in some major research study, but built would appear to be vitally important as a protection for the child.

Without guilt, the working mother might not rush out of the office at 5 p.m. or 6 p.m. when her colleagues are all staying for an after-hours meeting or drink – because she wants to be home for supper and bathtime with her children. Without guilt, the highly ambitious and motivated career woman might work at weekends as well as all the week, letting her children be looked after by a nanny or babysitter – when all the children want is some time with Mummy.

Without guilt, in fact, women might become like men. Heaven help us!

Many women I spoke to described the crucial difference between the ways they and men operate the dual function in their lives. Men don't seem to worry, if they work till 9 p.m. most evenings, that they are denying their child its birthright. They feel they can make up the time by spending all day Saturday, for example, with the children. The majority of men do not feel their children will suffer from a lack of their daily attention. Relationships, to men, tend to operate on that level – whether it's with their female partners, children or business associates. They lack the gut-level, umbilical-type attachment women feel.

KEEPING UP WITH A CHANGING WORLD

Two American child psychiatrists, in a recent book devoted to a study of children's behaviour and personalities, *Know Your Child*, make interesting comments about the changes that have been taking place regarding young children and mothers returning to work. Drs Stella Chess and Alexander Thomas, of the New York University Medical Center (for a further discussion of their views see also Chapter 12), argue favourably for the successful raising of healthy children by working mothers.

They conclude with some fascinating statements and questions about our lives today. For example, about the conflicts women still suffer when trying to establish their careers while remaining good mothers:

> Are they unrealistic, even in these days, in worrying that pregnancy and childbearing may represent a hazard to a woman's career? Will she lose promotion or a chance for a new job because she will be considered 'handicapped' by pregnancy and then by being the mother of a young infant? These are real, objective concerns for career women, and we have known a number who have anguished seriously and realistically over this problem. For a man, of course, fatherhood does not pose this kind of potential threat; it does not jeopardize his competitive job position ...
>
> If anything career women have to be capable of especially clear judgements of role boundaries. Otherwise, they will find it more difficult to manage simultaneously their work and household responsibilities ... Women do continue to agonise over their choices: domestic motherhood versus working outside the home; marriage versus single living; one versus several children; working as a necessity to maintain a decent family standard of living versus not working and accepting a lower family income. And these women receive no help from many mental health professionals who are still bound to the sexist concept, evidence or not, that a mother's place is in the home.

How do women confront the hard choices that face them? How do they decide about work, career and motherhood?

It was interesting to discover these questions posed by eminent child psychiatrists, which mirror my own basic questions.

ANGER AT MALE COLLEAGUES AND THE MALE-DOMINATED WORKPLACE

Many of the sections in the book appear to be fuelled by an ill-concealed anger against the men whom working mothers are confronting in the workplace. Few of the women I interviewed are card-carrying feminists. It's likely they cannot afford to be as heavy political commitment would make them appear difficult to work with, and not at all likely to fit in 'at the top'.

But their anger is still a predominant refrain. Which is why I felt that a discussion that took place with a male senior executive of an important company is valuable here. Although I will obviously disguise its identity, the company is one that employs and promotes a lot of women. The man I will call Michael is in no way speaking for all men, in all companies, as he began apologetically, 'I'm fairly untypical of most men, in that I like women and enjoy working with them.'

Unlike the average male, indeed, he was able to be painfully honest and excessively truthful. Within his words and attitudes I think we can learn a lot about other men, their views, feelings, neuroses and fears. Once, as a woman, we have decided to enter their world, on male terms, we have agreed implicitly (yet again) to understand, sympathise, make allowances for, even nurture – just as in the past women perfected their role as wives – the male in the working world.

Michael is responsible for a workforce of over one hundred. Of those men and women, several senior positions are held by women – but none are right at the top. Nevertheless, it is an industry in which women can, and do, succeed. Asked about his views of the time women take off for children, his attitude is that today's professional women take the statutory maternity leave, or even less.

They know the very nature of the job imposes a need for them to be there. As far as he is concerned, thay take off the bare minimum and then rush back to work.

Michael does not feel his female colleagues miss out on the promotion stakes because of having children. But he does think that their salaries should take into account the fact they are going to pay a nanny, or other substitute person, for childcare. That's not to say they'd be paid more than a man in a similar position. But certainly they should not be paid less.

If the salary is good, he maintains, then the woman with young children will have peace of mind, and will produce better quality work. He recognises that working mothers often work less 'in-office' hours, making up at evenings and weekends. 'Or, they put in the same sort of hours as before and settle for being a "bad" mother,' he quipped.

A MALE BOSS'S VIEW OF THE WOMAN EXECUTIVE

I've worked all my adult life with a number of women, and I have to say that for the type of work we do here women really are the best. In the field of communications, dealing with other people, women are the best because they are nurturers. They nurture their clients just as they do their children. Why are they the best? Because they are the most passionately committed, worrying what will happen next type of workers. They *mind* tremendously – unless they're overcompensating for being women and appear hard, brittle, too ambitious and grasping.

Does that mean I would employ a woman rather than a man for that type of position? Maybe. I wouldn't like to think of it that way. Only that most often women do seem to *be* the best candidates. I find it intriguing and exciting, in fact, to be surrounded by dominant, intelligent and demanding women. Intelligent women turn me on.

But that's me. There's another type of male who doesn't like intelligent, strong, dominant women. He just doesn't know what to do with them. I've seen it happen: they'd rather they didn't exist. You know the type, they tend to be married to submissive women themselves. They can only cope with women who flirt, or whom they can dominate. The appearance of the intelligent or strong woman drives them into a frenzy. In certain types of work, women are supposed to behave like men; they become 'female men', one of the guys. Maybe she's managing a team of 8–10, many of whom are men, who really feel she ought to be a man. It's just a shame she's a woman.

A lot of men I know will touch a woman – absolutely wrongly – in the office. They'll be talking to a woman who is their equal at work and they put their arms around her and say 'Hello, darling'. I've watched women in that situation freeze. But a really strong woman doesn't take it. She finds that kind of behaviour a gross put-down and usually walks away, or she'll treat him with his own grossness and call him 'dear' or 'darling' in return. You should see the look of amazement on that man's face to be called 'dear'. He wouldn't even realise he's used that sort of language himself.

The type of woman who is rising to senior positions won't let herself be put down. I've told my own daughters that: never let yourself be put down by man or woman. That way you keep hold of yourself – of your confidence and credibility. Women who let themselves be put down just won't make it to the top. Because they've given in and done what the men wanted. They've lost the battle before they've begun.

But there is one area where the average male employer will feel uncomfortable with women who are his equals. It's hard to get around this one. If he has to, he can tell another man to go 'fuck off' or 'shut up'. But I wouldn't speak the same way to a senior woman. The first phrase I wouldn't use, the second I couldn't use. Five minutes later I'd be opening the door for her. There's a feeling of diffidence in such relationships. At the same time, the woman must feel a similar diffidence with the men she works with. This can make some women overreact to become overly hard and strong, I think, in self-defence.

Just how some of these successful women are as wives at home, I don't know. They might be earning more than their men. They're used to behaving at work as rapaciously strong, determined to succeed, and very often playing every card as downright attractive women, too. The husbands must have to be very very patient and generous to be able to take it.

There's one area I must confess that I have a very unreconciled position on: I could not imagine working with a male secretary. I just don't think I'd employ one. I remember being shocked going into an office and seeing a young man secretary at the typewriter, taking dictation. The women who have worked for me as secretaries have also always been intelligent and strong-minded. Usually older women. Yet, by not wanting to see a man in this position, I appear to be expecting, wanting, to have a female servant, don't I?

2 IS THIS RIGHT FOR ME, AND FOR MY CHILD?

We met for lunch as soon as the early pregnancy nausea had faded sufficiently, so she once again desired food and time spent in restaurants. A magazine editor, now four months pregnant, she was excited about her pregnancy but at the same time expressing her fears and doubts.

What sort of arrangement was she going to make at work about maternity leave and returning? I asked the question very simply, never assuming she would not be fitting motherhood in with her work life. Most women these days, particularly if they have a good, interesting and reasonably well-paying job, do make these adjustments.

But I had overestimated her ability to make the leap at this stage of the pregnancy. Nearly 32 years old, expecting her first child, she was unsure what decision she was going to make. 'I could work from home, freelance articles,' she began saying, a frown appearing visibly on the hormonally permeated, newly radiant skin. 'That's not as easy as it sounds', was my response spoken from years of hard-won experience. 'Why not stay with the job?'

The issues we were skirting gently around that lunchtime affect all women at this one crucial point in their lives. When they become mothers are they to continue with their careers? As I mentioned earlier, to a degree the collective guilt in society has vanished. Women no longer feel constrained by the male-held view that we ought to be at home for at least five years.

But that does not override female-held feelings: the emotional doubts, the concern that full-time work is maybe

too many hours to be giving to a workplace, too few for your
child. Part-time work, job-sharing, self-employment, starting
up your own business: I doubt there is a working mother who
has not given these options some thought.

But, the thought acknowledged, immediately the other part
of the equation springs into view: once you drop out of the
system of 'mainstream career', any form of re-entry will be
that much harder in future years. Just think about all the
women in previous decades who swallowed the line – they
could take five years out to raise their children and could then
slide back into the workforce. Whatever happened to them?
They ended up their years running dress shops, selling home-
made jams, or went back into teaching or nursing (at the
lowest grade and salary levels). That's not what we are
expecting or feel we deserve today.

Being honest and frank with themselves most women know
they will probably never make up the lost time in terms of
position, seniority, promotion and salary. Even when a mere
few months are taken as maternity leave, there may be a
struggle to make up not only lost time, but lost prestige and
battling points.

When a woman worker becomes a mother, to the eyes of
most of the male work world (still), she is no longer a fighter
on their terms. Her place on the ladder has been removed. As
one businesswoman put it:

> The image of a manager, in the corporate world, is very much in
> the role of the male warrior, a fighter. Managerial ability tends to be
> measured by hours put in, obstacles run through, and sang-froid
> in being able to fire those weaker mortals who can't take the pace!

The magazine editor, meanwhile, had remembered the
story of a young woman with a high-powered position in a
merchant bank. The hours expected of those young whizz
kids, the 100 per cent loyalty to their work, made it impossible
for any woman to continue once she became pregnant.

> They pay you off handsomely. Sufficiently so to prevent you
> taking action through a sex discrimination tribunal. But they just

don't want women with children around. So they force you out. My friend told me she couldn't make up her mind whether to have a child or not. What a decision to have to make ...! If she took the money and left, she'd have to find some other form of work, begin a new career while her child was young.

But do women want to fight on these male terms? Do they want success at work over more personal, life-fulfilling successes? Or is the very nature of the question itself unfairly loaded against women – when men do not have to make such choices?

If a woman gives up, opts out, moves sideways, is that a reflection of defeat – or that she has her head screwed on in a more well-adjusted way? Such major decisions to be made ... what woman can know, until she has tried, which path suits her best? There have been so many battles lost along the way.

As the magazine editor said, very quietly, waking up to this new idea (it's a lesson most mothers learn along with that rush of milk into the breasts):

I really believed there was equality by now at work. Not totally. I wasn't that naive. But, once you become pregnant, your eyes become wide open to the fact there isn't. Worse is the fact no one really seems to care what happens to you and your career. They more or less write you off.

Most male colleagues assumed she wouldn't return. But, in a heavily female-dominated industry, her worst problems were with women bosses:

Either they're single and resentful, or, they only returned to work after ten years raising their children – and think you should do the same. Worst of all are the ones who resolutely worked right through motherhood, and left their children with a nanny for twelve hours a day. They jump on the defensive if you so much as hint your own child might need to see more of you in its early months!

WORKING MOTHER NEEDS AT-HOME 'WIFE' SUPPORT

The economies of the debate are also paramount. A woman has to be earning sufficiently well to afford decent childcare to make any return to full-time professional work even thinkable. Any form of such work involves attitudes of mind and hours that are inflexible. Although there are childminders and the occasional nursery place available, most women in senior positions recognise they need the full-time support of a nanny, babysitter, housekeeper, relative, or whomever can supply the full-time substitute care of a full-time mother.

It's been said before – working mothers need the services and support of a good, traditional, old-fashioned, 'at-home' wife. During my research, it became obvious, with a certain sick irony, that once again the women most likely to succeed – in a strange mirror image of women's previous status – require supportive, kind, and *wealthy* husbands (or at least well heeled and generous enough to fund the 'substitute caregiver's' wages). When the dice are loaded, a woman needs a strong, successful marriage to a good, successful man. Without the care, willingness to help finance the situation and agreement on sharing certain duties regarding the child, or housekeeping, a working mother may find herself up against the wall in an unending and maybe self-defeating struggle.

But that is not to say single mothers, or women whose husbands are not supportive, kind, generous, etc., necessarily give up or fail. Far from it. I have heard some great, inspiring and couragous stories (indeed I had no such plain sailing myself) from women who have managed, survived and fought their battles alone. But it has to be said that those who have the easiest time, who suffer less guilt, least exhaustion, and ultimately may even win most respect from male colleagues, have the proverbial 'good man' behind them.

WHAT SORT OF WOMEN BECOME 'CAREER MOTHERS'?

So many different women. So many different stories. One thing we learn early in researching a project such as this: there is an endless variety of views, opinions, plans, ambitions, dreams, fears and levels of enjoyment to take into account.

I shall begin by bringing in a cross-section of the types of responses I received to the knotty question 'How do you handle your career with motherhood?' As suggested in Chapter 1, the topic is basically still so 'hot', controversial, debatable and likely to set women off into defensive arguments about their own stance that I felt it best to give every one an airing, so the broad spectrum of the discussion becomes the basis for the rest of the book.

There is little advice one woman can give another on this basic philosophical starting point to their lives. In fact, most women have learned to close their ears to such advice. Long ago their own mothers might have said, 'Surely you won't be going back to work so soon?' Neighbours and colleagues may have implied that being a working mother is somehow wrong. If they have already decided to override such criticism, then they are by definition already independent-minded, determined to follow their own resolve. But, as you will see, they still vary very much in their fundamental attitudes.

DETERMINED TO GO BACK AFTER FIGHTING FOR HER POSITION

Jane is 32, a very bright, ambitious, female manager of one of the leading City branches of a national building society. When first we met, she was heavily pregnant, about to give birth and go on maternity leave. She was grappling with most of the major issues such an event means to a woman's life — both to her working, and her emotional or spiritual, life. Now her son is a few weeks old:

I'd planned to take off sixteen weeks — I had about nine days before he was born – and I've negotiated to go back three days a week for three months to the twenty-nine-week point (of legally entitled maternity leave). The three-day week may make finding a nanny harder, but it will give me a chance to adjust to the duality of my role.

The truth is that very few females reach managerial level in this industry, because it takes eight years to reach that mark. If you came in as a graduate at 22, many will have chosen to leave for marriage and children before they make the grade. The building society industry has been notoriously *dull*, and unforward-looking. I don't think it has been attracting the right type of go-ahead women either. When you think about all these men making decisions for someone like myself. Their stereotypes are their wives who've stayed home to bring up *their* children.

So I'm working now on making my company more enlightened. We employ 80 per cent female staff, but mostly at the clerical level. When I finally announced my pregnancy, they *assumed* I wouldn't be coming back. But I'm determined to go back, having fought to get where I am. I'm not giving it all up now.

At the moment my bosses are in a state of shock! I'm determined to shake them up a little. Because of our huge branch network, there is really no opportunity for women to meet each other and compare notes. So I plan to work on a booklet for all the women in the company, to get our maternity leave provision sorted out.

At my senior level, for instance, they were going to treat me like a clerk/cashier. They were planning to take away my staff rate mortgage, to replace it with the normal rate. And to take away my company car for the sixteen weeks' maternity leave! It's pretty insulting – for someone at senior management level. But, apart from that, they've really been very good and understanding, once they overcame the initial shock!

Ellen, 35, is in a very enviable position, in almost total control of a company employing nearly one hundred people. She is also mother to two girls who are now 8 and 5 years old, and stepmother to two teenage daughters. As she sees the situation today, it is almost the norm for women to stay on at work, once they have children:

It's sort of unusual for the women here, at least, to definitely declare they're *not* coming back. Almost no one says to me, 'I'm having a baby and I'll be leaving.' They come to discuss maternity leave, hours, and how they plan to make it work. We're quite liberal and tolerant here. I do think women on the whole are more serious about their careers than they have ever been before. And they worry about where they've got to, or why they're not getting there.

Ellen has done very well in her own field. For her, motherhood has not come between herself and advancement. Only last year, when she was unexpectedly fired from her previous position and was out of work for three months, she was inundated with offers of new jobs.

It was a great shock being laid off like that. And I decided to take time to think about what sort of position I wanted next. I went for several interviews and finally accepted this position – as managing director of the company – because it gives me far more administrative responsibility than I'd been used to. This was an area I wished to develop in my own career.

During those three months out of work, I gradually developed a vision that I had the capacity for a more managerial role. Originally I graduated with an arts degree – but now I feel very fulfilled as I'm dealing with the financial side, personnel and even chair our board meetings, although I never received any formal training in management.

I do work hard and I made it clear from the start that I would be leaving work at 5.30 p.m. as my children are still young. I tend to be rushing out of the building close to six, and spend a lot of money on taxis getting home. I've known friends who are working mothers, who stay in the office till 8 p.m. But I won't do that. I won't have dinner or drinks with people after work. I do tea instead. Breakfast meetings are worse, because my children accept that I'm away between 9 a.m.–6 p.m., but they go berserk if I do something that takes up the early morning, or the weekend. I manage to take our elder daughter to school before work.

Both girls know I work because I *want* to. I make no pretence about it being just for the money, though, as I am a second wife, we do need my income. I want to give them a role model of women doing something because they *want* to. My own mother worked intermittently, but she never had a 9 to 5 job.

MAKING A CHANGE FROM THEIR MOTHERS' WAY OF LIFE

Whether the mother in question was a sedate, unquestioning housewife, or a rather bitter woman strung along by society, trying desperately to make ends meet, many find it easy to accept that they do not want to live out their mothers' previous-generation style of existence.

Naomi, for example, a 36-year-old woman working within the civil service in ethnic affairs, is the product of an inter-racial marriage who grew up in very tense times in the 1950s. Married, and the mother of a 2-year-old son, she is honest about her desire to get on and succeed – not as a black woman, but as a woman.

> The whole business of working to me was always very important. My mother worked hard, she was a machinist, a sweatshop worker who suffered from lack of planning, fear of education and because she was caught between two cultures.
>
> So I was determined, when we had our child, to deal with being a working mother. My husband and I both work, and we share the taking and collecting of our son to the childminder. Although I leave earlier in the afternoons than some of my colleagues, I achieve targets by working at weekends and late two nights a week.
>
> Besides, I don't believe only I can give my son everything he needs. The more he's exposed to other people the better it is for him. I don't even like being with him for too long at a time. If I were to stay home twenty-four hours, I'd soon go nuts!

Anne, 41, a marketing manager with a major computer firm – mother of a 5-year-old daughter and a 2-year-old son – talked about coming late into her career, having started out on that rocky road chosen by so many from girlhood dreams of 'happiness' – that of marriage and a non-structured form of working.

She was married, at 20, to a man who travelled abroad a lot. Eventually Anne took up work as a secretary and also worked hard on doing up the big house they bought in a country area close to London.

It was only when I got divorced that I woke up to the fact no one was going to take my renovation of the house as anything other than a wifely duty! No mention of the organisation involved. And I realised then how unfair it all was. Because I had not worked, I was then 30 years old and not at all a marketable commodity.

I began working as a receptionist at a hotel. The work really wasn't at my level, but I'd lost such a lot of time I had to make it up very quickly. My career began with my present company, as a secretary/assistant. Soon I was moving up. I'm enormously determined, and very single-minded. I knew I was going to get to my level . . . I think I'm there now. But I'd like to go still further.

When I remarried, my husband is 14 years older, we both wanted children – so we had them in a short space of time. My husband understood I would continue working, and how much it means to me. He insisted we pay for a full-time nanny because he did not want the children to suffer. He is very, very supportive of me, and I know I'm lucky in that.

WHICH SHOULD COME FIRST: AMBITION OR FAMILY?

Certain forms of work demand long hours of their women and their men. If you're going to be part of that usually well-paying, dynamic, exciting, challenging work, as a woman and a mother, what can you do? As previously mentioned, some all-male industries either give women a subtle push or casually let the women push themselves out once they become mothers, because the answer to that question is so imponderable. As one woman said, in such an industry 'at senior level, the assumption is one's personal life is dispensable'.

But some women do manage to sustain both roles. Judy is a good example. Aged 32, with a daughter just under 1 year old, Judy continues to put in the long hours working for a major bank, a decision that is made easier because, as well as the full-time nanny, her actor husband is often at home.

I wasn't really involved in my career till quite late. I was 28 before I joined this company (one of the leading corporate banking

firms). I had always loved organising, but it never dawned on me
that I was so ambitious. Until then I'd worked as a student foreign
tour manager.

I usually leave the house by 7.15 a.m. and am at my desk by
8–8.15 a.m. I don't tend to see my daughter in the morning. One
evening a week I make sure I'm home by 6.30 p.m. But that's all. I
just would not be able to rush home at 5.30–6 p.m. every day. If I
wanted that way of life, then really I'd have to leave and find
another job. None of the men have proper family lives either.
There's certainly a lot of kids out there not seeing much of their
fathers. At least our daughter spends a lot of time with hers.

Many people told me I'd change my mind about my baby once
she was born. They warned me I'd want to stay home. But it was
quite the reverse. I took six months off, and physically I was glad
of that as I was in no fit state to return, which would have made
things worse, workwise. But after three months I was so desperate
for a break, that I booked us all tickets on a whim to Australia. I
felt completely ground down, tired, depressed – she was very
hungry, and fed all the time. I wasn't being recognised, I wasn't
being paid for this work. To me, it was crucifying. Now, I like the
balance. Though I didn't expect quite such a division between
work-life and motherhood.

Linda, now 37, director of a PR firm and mother of two
daughters aged 12 and 8, looks back and can see that –
although she has always worked and supported herself – for
years she did not notice how strong her own streak of
ambition was.

I'd been to a rather exclusive girls' school and came out like so
many not really focusing on anything. I'd always been a competitive horse rider, however, and I began writing a series of riding
articles which started me on my career because I came in touch
with journalism. By the time I was 28, and my elder daughter was
3, my first marriage had collapsed and I was forced to support
myself. I managed to get by on the freelancing – I paid the bills
and also supported this huge racer who was eating us out of house
and home.

I married again and had another daughter. That was a real
disaster. I've not been good at choosing men (until now, I hope, as
I've just remarried). He was manic-depressive and the respons-

ibility of it all sent him off the rails. The turning point for me was when the second marriage broke up and there I was with two children – the youngest was 2 – a horse and a dog. We were living in the country, and I happened to see an advert for a job at the Institute of Marketing in our local paper.

I thought I'd give it a couple of years full time, to see how that went. I found a very good childminder and lined up friends for a back-up system. I was determined never to say I was having a domestic crisis and that I had to go back home!

And since then I've never put family first. I demand good solid childcare and back-up systems. I've done very well and was recently made a director of the PR firm I'm now with. In a few years, I've become quite a marketable commodity, but I have refused to move up to London. This way I'm near the children. I work long days, often till 8.30 or 9 p.m., but I can be home in five minutes.

I love my children dearly, but I have to be honest and say I get more enjoyment from the job than from playing with them. I don't think that's made me a bad mother. But I do know that a career is about commitment; it's no different from the commitment a man makes. There shouldn't be one rule for us and one for them.

COMPROMISING – TO BE FAIR TO THE FAMILY

Some women have tried both worlds, endeavouring to blend a less structured work-life with the early years of motherhood. Then, ultimately, they have found a niche in the full-time market. The change can bring greater rewards in fulfilment, self-confidence and financially. But the hours involved may well hurt.

Maryanne, now 40, whose children are 9 and 7, originally worked on newspapers, but became a freelance writer when her son was born.

Ten years ago, when I started freelancing, I thought it would be the perfect way to carry on a career while the children were young. Of course, I didn't realise until I was really too far into parenthood, and this particular career path, that this form of work is as difficult as any independent business, without outside supports and guidelines, can be. I was working harder and making less. The need to support myself financially led to many weekends and evenings of work, which complicated the home domestic scene (especially when my husband also decided to turn freelance for a few years).

'Keeping up' in my business meant many lunches, meetings and phone contacts for which I was not paid, and for which I had to find the 'extra' time. Daycare for the children was not easy either.

Now that I am finally back on a real career track (working on one of the national dailies), I do find the hours very draining. Some 'star' writers get to work from home, and to be completely independent. But most page editors are expected to be here daily, and to work a day full to overflowing. I have begun to miss some of those hours I could spend with the children. And although they are both in school, I have found the after-school care just as difficult as when they were younger.

However, due to a change in production schedules, I can now come in early at 7.30 a.m. and leave by 3.30 p.m. or so. I'm rid of the afternoon sitter, and have time with the children at home, which is a relief. My husband, fortunately, can look after them in the morning before he goes off to work.

There are compromises one must make in order to be fair to the family. I can't really say I'd have been any happier without the juggling and baggage I now have! With my new income we can at least afford our move out of the city; the big house with its lovely garden. The children all appreciate it needs my working to help pay for that.

IT IS ONLY DEFEAT IF YOU LOOK IN MALE TERMS

For someone like Sarah, nearly 38 with two children aged 5 and 2, an accountant with a major company, career has always been very important. But motherhood has forced her to change her views on the question of what hours and pressures at work are tolerable.

The pressures that led to a near crack-up for Sarah may eventually drive her out of the company altogether into, as she says, 'who knows what, just something different' – where she can use her talents and fit work into hours that suit both herself and her children.

I have a very high tolerance level for suffering, but at one point last year I nearly cracked under the strain. The way the company treated me, when I returned from my second pregnancy, changed my whole attitude to them. In itself, that was self-defeating because, in order to succeed, you have to look after your career development. In effect, I coasted for a while and let my skills drop.

I was working for very difficult men; some of them were notorious! Then suddenly I was put in a very high pressure job, with very long hours. Because my technical skills had slipped, and my bosses were very unsupportive, this led to an extreme level of stress.

Maybe some women could cope with the pressures, but I couldn't. I was not getting home till 7 p.m. at the earliest. I'd often have to work out a patchwork of substitute care to give my nanny her time off. To make matters worse, my husband was travelling most of that time, and neither of my children have been good sleepers. For a period of five years, in fact, it has not been unusual for my sleep to be broken three or five times a night!

I never made a fuss at work about my lack of sleep. I always imagined they'd just hear it as a 'female' whinge. But when the nanny then said she was leaving, and I was under this stress at work, my mind and body had obviously had enough. What man can know the feeling – trying to find a new nanny, keeping up working, worrying about your children?

Finally, my husband woke up to what was happening when I put a carton of eggs on the gas and lit the flame under them! That stressful time has helped me analyse my own strengths and weaknesses, and prompted me to do something about the situation.

It's not motherhood *per se* that has changed my career plans, but things that have happened to me along the way. The attitudes of people around me. Having had to take stock of the situation has broadened my horizons dramatically. Motherhood and the children in fact have broadened my 'life' horizons.

AT WHAT PRICE HAVE WOMEN ENTERED THE MALE WORLD?

Sarah went on to describe the type of situation that traps women in the working world. She identifies it as when women turn into 'female chaps'. Women who don't have children go to the pub after hours, they talk like the men, even think like the men. It forces them into accepting the male ideal, and often into selling out on other women friends or colleagues; certainly into the notion of putting family firmly into second place: 'I'm not a female chap any more, and a lot of other things are important to me. We women shouldn't lose sight of the fact we have a sense of balance in our lives that men don't have.'

Whether her form of stepping sideways is an admission of defeat or failure is, nevertheless, still a question that vexes Sarah.

> It's only admitting defeat if you measure life in terms of the male world. Part of me does think it's a 'failure', but only when I'm in their world. When I'm away from it, I can see more clearly – 'who the hell wants to do that kind of work, with that level of stress, for the rest of their life anyway?'
>
> I'd prefer now to have my own business, to juggle the time I spend with the children on my own terms. I'd be more committed and involved in the work that way. I do enjoy accountancy, and I know I could run a business, along the consultancy lines, in which I would help people understand the mysteries of bookkeeping and numbers. It's typical that women would be the ones to take up that form of consultancy work, isn't it?

This question of hours and the sort of commitment demanded of both men and women at work today proves a volatile debating point. As one woman said, 'They expect you there for them twenty-four hours a day.' But the vexing question is whether women are going to be able to change the hours situation through their own example, working less strenuous hours for the sake of their children. Or whether the reverse pattern has already set in whereby women, as well as men, will continue vying for pride of place working eighty-plus-hour weeks.

Celia, aged 42, with one daughter of 11 and a second baby under 1 year old, has reached a position in her particular field as a designer where she is in demand, can work from home, and can also choose her hours – all with admirable remuneration into the bargain.

I was 30 when I had my first baby, working for a company which needed me. I was able to negotiate to come back to do a three-day week. My husband was freelancing from home and not earning very much, so we in fact split the parenting responsibilities three and a half days a week each. Really it was the ideal situation. I did three long days in the office, but I never had to worry about our daughter because she was with her other parent.

I believed then – back in the idealistic seventies – that both men and women were working towards this *equally*: shared parenting and shorter working hours. But it seems as though we're moving towards the opposite: long hours, very competitive situations at work. I read recently of a mother returning to full-time work when her baby was only 10 days old. I found that really depressing.

Women do seem to have succeeded in entering the man's world – but at what price? Have they only won that place by playing the man's game? I don't now know if change will come about. At the same time, I see a political drive to force women back into the home. Either they accept these working conditions, or they leave. Cruel, isn't it?

But then Dee, who works in publishing – a more female-dominated (though male-ruled) industry – reports that only two years ago, when her son was born, she was able to bring him in as a newborn and breastfeed at her desk.

CAN WE STRIKE A HAPPY BALANCE BETWEEN WORK AND FAMILY?

One of the major questions that emerges throughout this book is that of balance. Is there a happy balance to be struck between work and family? Can women achieve success, fulfilment, happiness from a career, even in a male-dominated field, and feel they are giving enough time to their children, to themselves, to their marriages or other interests?

Are women compromising themselves, their children or their ambitions? Which comes first? Which should go first?

These are the issues of our age. Women today are living exemplars of just what might be a better future; or a worse one for our daughters and sons.

Joanna Foster, the new commissioner of the Equal Opportunities Commission (EOC), wonders whether the 'divided loyalties' issue belongs only in the hearts of women? Women do not want to become male clones. They are concerned about the quality of life, and do want very much to 'have it all': meaning an interesting work life, and a valuable family experience.

Most of women's career patterns do not mirror those of men. My own is quite typical of my generation: what I call a patchwork, as for years I followed my husband around pursuing his career. But women today are helping free men from rigid patterns. Men are refusing to move for jobs that will unnecessarily disrupt their family life, for example. I do believe men privately are talking about 'what price success?'

Companies, and all employers, are going to have to think of what they can offer both men and women today. By the age of 28, any woman is likely to be thinking 'What am I going to do about my life as well as my career?' Can I fit in kids with my career right now? If I leave it later what will the physical problems be? If I leave it later will I be more valuable to the company and thereby offset any physical problems? If I have a child how would I reorganise my life?'

WOMEN ARE NEEDED, AS NEVER BEFORE, IN THE WORKFORCE

Fortunately, for the situation of women, we are now in a more powerful position *vis-à-vis* the workforce. There is a skills shortage, a decreasing recruitment pool, and employers in certain areas of the country are desperate to take on, and keep, their most valued female employees. This, if nothing else, will force some changes into the workplace.

The labour market is threatened with contraction, as today's baby-boomers finish producing their children and a much smaller pool of young people becomes ready to enter the work-force. All over Europe and the United States, women's organisations are noticing the first signs of change. Companies, even large corporations, just might have to adapt their rigid policies to keep their women employees. Work and family life is likely to become the big issue of the 1990s. Already certain trail-blazing companies have seen the situation as an opportunity to show just how 'sensitive' they are to modern needs.

An American economist and writer summed up the situation in a recent issue of *Working Mother*, in an article entitled 'Can you make it to the top – and still be a good parent':

> The demographic changes that point to a shrinking labour pool increasingly dominated by women have awakened corporations to the need to accommodate working families. To attract and keep the best and the brightest, companies may be forced to change the work environment from a macho one to a more humanistic one. Along with childcare benefits, corporate work/family task forces are discussing more flexible work hours, work-at-home options and the utilisation of more part-time workers.
>
> Such changes will ease the pressures for entry-level and middle managers. But competition for the highest-paid senior posts remains keen. At the top, change may be longer in coming, if it comes at all. As long as there are ambitious managers who will-ingly sacrifice family life for career advancement, life at the top, or near it, will be relentlessly demanding and frequently all-consuming.

JUST BECAUSE YOU WORK HALF A WEEK, DOESN'T MEAN YOU HAVE HALF A BRAIN

A highly successful partner in a business founded by herself and her husband, Sophia come up with one of the most logical and outspoken statements about her *modus vivendi* in defence of solid, respectable, high-status, part-time work, geared particularly to mothers of children. Sophia has been able to make use of such part-time work in her own life, and is now helping other women follow suit. Her ideas are certainly illuminating.

Now 42, mother of two teenage daughters, and in her own right a millionaire, Sophia's major comment on the issue of flexibility of hours and the balance or quality of life for women is:

Just because you work half a week, doesn't mean you only have half a brain.

I had been in a variety of careers before meeting my husband and immediately we had our two children. What happens to women like me? We fall in love, have one or two babies, and lose out on the network and career ladder. Because I was finally able to find work myself with a major company, who employed sales agents on a part-time basis, when we set up our own company I went out of my way deliberately to employ educated women with children who want to work part-time hours.

I know these women give me full-time devotion, loyalty and commitment. They're far better workers than the average full-time male. Most large companies just refuse to understand or see their value. But if you analyse the way most people spend their time in offices, a lot of it is 'downtime': chatting, drinking coffee, travelling to and from meetings or appointments. When you phone the sales manager and learn she's not available, what difference does it make if she's home peeling potatoes, picking up the children from school or sitting in a high-powered conference in Geneva? Who would know?

My management team is highly successful. It means I can be more in control, and they are happy to work for us because they don't have to commit 9–5 Monday–Friday to an office. Basically I think women are far better workers than men, anyway.

There's a 'people revolution' going on. Recently, as our company was being floated on the stock market, I had the experience of sitting in on high-powered meetings with merchant bankers and lawyers. We were there all day and evening, until 11.30 p.m. Two or three were women, the rest were men. I watched the charade: 90 per cent of it was ritualistic posturing.

And afterwards one of the women, the lawyer's assistant, said, 'If there'd just been two or three women we could have finished in half the time.' It's a changing world, and I really do believe things will begin to shift for both men and women.

I know too many men, in their mid-40s, who have been ambitious and successful. Now, quite young, they're MDs of companies and they're saying, 'I've got here, and I'm bored'. What is life all about if we have the quantity but not the quality? What's the point in working ninety-hour weeks?

It all began for me when I had my two young children and I tried to get back into sales management. I was offered jobs but I refused to work five days. All I was asking for was one day a week off. No one would grant it. They were afraid of the very concept. But I couldn't leave my children with someone else all week. Not only would I have to pay that person, but manage all that extra responsibility too.

So just where will the individual woman or man find a position in this changing picture? There is so much for all of us to decide upon – emotionally and spiritually – in terms of demands from children, partners and from our overall view of the quality of life. We hear that much in society might be changing – yet might not.

Success is important. Ambition is fine. Aggression is no longer unfeminine – but families need and deserve time.

3 SWINGS AND ROUNDABOUTS: PLUSES AND MINUSES OF CAREER/MOTHERHOOD

Stress is a male-loaded term we seldom use in association with women – other than in banal jokes about how tough it can be looking after children. And working mothers are often their own worst enemies in keeping quiet about some of the difficulties they encounter, lest the rest of the workforce (particularly their male colleagues) begin to suspect they really cannot cope

Though, ultimately, just as with the issue of who provides for the 'substitute mothercare', I do believe women have a right to be guarded about the emotional or psychological problems they encounter, such fear and defensiveness may sometimes be self-defeating. But then who could possibly understand, other than maybe another career-mother? Who would not fail to judge her badly if she confessed in the office to exhaustion, battle fatigue or burn-out? The door often seems to be wide open, offering women the way out – back into the home and the traditional lifestyle of full-time motherhood.

But it is time to bring out some of the stress or burn-out issues into the open, if for no other reason than to help other women realise that many of the seemingly insurmountable problems can be resolved or cured. First, we have to stop turning our heads away; stop burying them deeper and deeper in the sand.

Research scientists have finally begun to study working

mothers as a useful pool of high-stressed guinea pigs for their data. In a recent article in the *New York Times*, for example, research was reported from the cardiovascular unit at the New York Hospital–Cornell Medical Center. Some 120 technical and clerical workers were wired up to record their stress levels throughout the work-day and their time at home in the evenings. Women in low-paid, or low-responsibility jobs, who then go home to family and domestic responsibilities, are at especially high risk for going over the top on these stress charts.

Comparing their findings with that of a stockbroker in one of the major finance houses on October 1987's Black Monday, the hospital secretary/administrative assistant chosen for this test registered higher on the stress machine than the man whose career and perhaps life-savings were falling down at his feet. Most interestingly, her stress levels not only shot up during the anxieties and aggravations of the work-day, but went even higher during the aggravations of the evening, when she was dealing with two teenage children and a somewhat chauvinistic and unsupportive husband.

By comparison, the stockbroker, despite the tensions of that dramatic day, went home to watch television with his wife. With no other pressing responsibilities, his blood pressure dropped rapidly.

By dinner-time, the working mother's blood pressure was higher than it had been all day at the office. She had forgotten a ballet class for her daughter, tried to organise for another parent to take her next week, had to help her son with his homework, prepare dinner, do the laundry, change sheets on beds, etc. Worse was an argument with her husband over the daughter's activities for the coming weekend.

This working mother told the reporter that she felt guilty for her children's sake because she could see they were upset at her being out at work all day.

> I'm not always there when the children want me around, and it bothers me, so I make a special effort to take them around and find things for them to do at the weekends. I don't want them to get bored. It's not their fault I have to work to make a living.

She recognised that her guilt levels were maybe unnecessarily high.

These problems were identified as part of women's 'dual-role conflict'. At the same time, it has been proven that women who work outside the home, and who have children, tend to be slightly healthier on average than those who stay home all day as full-time mothers. Depression, boredom, frustration and lack of strong self-image afflict the stay-at-home mother with potentially more long-term emotional consequences.

Nevertheless, it is obvious that women struggling on alone, without a supportive husband, or even an easy-going relationship, who are taking on the burden of guilt for their children, and also taking on the full responsibility for domestic and household duties, are in danger of entering the burn-out zone.

That one piece of research focused on women in low-paying jobs who obviously cannot afford full childcare or household help. But others have noticed equally strong elements of stress in working mothers who are in high-flying careers. These women are the ones classified as Type E – meaning they abide by the formula of 'being everything to everybody'.

Psychologist and management consultant Harriet Braiker, in her book *Getting Up When You're Feeling Down: A Woman's Guide to Overcoming and Preventing Depression*, believes that stress is rife among mothers who work, particularly among those who are used to a level of competence and control in their working lives. They find it very hard to delegate; hard to say no to extra demands; and hard not to be the consistent paragon of self-reliant virtue.

'The more you demonstrate how much you can do, the more others demand of you . . . you become the victim of your own dazzling abilities,' she says. But, we should also hold on to the fine distinction between 'good' and 'bad' stress. Good stress leads to excitement, motivation, purpose and enthusiasm. Very often the above-mentioned 'dual-role conflict' can be a positive form of stress.

The bad side includes feelings of undue pressure, tension, frustration or the sense of there not being enough of you to go around. Both stress elements should be distinguished as separate from feelings of depression. If you're tired, exhausted or feel overloaded, that is still different from feeling sad, unhappy or unable to express pleasure in your life.

By making the mistake of becoming overly self-reliant, expecting ourselves to do everything and, as a consequence, resenting those we live and/or work with, many women are afraid that if we ask for help, it will seem as if we are nagging. Worse, we fear the request will be met with resistance.

Dr Braiker suggests tackling the problem as we would a business negotiation. Obviously, we are hoping someone else will accept full responsibility for a certain task, and thereby lighten our load. The other person, in turn, may see her or his self-interest best served by continuing to have *you* do the work. What is needed, therefore, is an acceptable compromise.

Begin by stating that you are no longer willing to do the chore – whether it's cooking dinner or handling the company's expense reports – unassisted all the time. This should be clearly defined as a non-negotiable position. The next step is to determine what, if anything, the other person might want in return for his aid.

Your goal is to strike a mutually acceptable deal through which you will get more help than you currently receive. You'll find that your husband, children, work colleagues and others will be more receptive to the idea of a negotiated contract than to repeated nagging or a hostile confrontation. Be honest – explain that your purpose is to reduce the stress levels in your life, with the intention of improving your mood.

ARE YOU APPRECIATED AT HOME OR AT WORK?

In the questionnaire I sent to those women willing or interested to become involved in the research for this book (which you will find reprinted in the Appendix), I asked whether they felt they were appreciated for what they were doing at work, and at home. There was a wide variety of responses – reflecting mostly the seniority of position the woman held at work, and the type of relationship she had with her husband (or the type of man he is). But the particular responses held the clue to each individual woman's self-esteem and overall level of 'good' or 'bad' stress.

Naomi, for example, the 32-year-old black woman who states that she and her husband share the problems involved with childcare, comments on the need for her to feel his equal involvement:

> Some men are very keen at the beginning, with a new baby, but they soon slacken off and leave everything to the woman again. My husband knows that's not on for me. He is continually supportive. I also have several outside commitments with black arts groups, and he usually stays home with our son when I'm out. Thankfully, ours is not a competitive relationship.
>
> However, I do notice that when my husband has spent a lot of time with our son, he needs a lot of vocal gratitude from me. He'll still say, 'I've done this for you.' If he were a wife he wouldn't expect any praise, thanks or gratitude, would he?

COMPETING GUILTS – AND CONFLICTING LOYALTIES

Levels of appreciation – for the work we do, the responsibilities taken on, and for the amount of stress or anxiety involved in both – are important to all of us. It is quite common for working mothers, in full-blown careers, to fall into the trap of fearing they are not succeeding either at home or at work. These successful, apparently 'doing-it-all', women will disarmingly tell you about their levels of 'failure'.

For some, this form of tension emerges as chronic guilt. Gillian, at 37, mother of a 3-year-old daughter, is one of the consortium of owners of a successful multimillion pound business. On paper, at least, she is a millionaire. Strikingly good-looking, and fun-loving in her attitude, Gillian might appear the living example of today's 'superwoman'. But to hear it from *her* lips, Gillian is far from 'super' anything:

I think I suffer from competing guilts. As women we're spurred on by guilt anyway, but the guilt over my child wins overall. I feel hugely guilty leaving her with a nanny all day. Also I don't feel appreciated at home which is a constant source of stress. I don't make a thing about my motherhood or perceived problems at work, and I don't want the women working for me to bring their mothering concerns into the office either.

Sometimes I feel I'd like to retire – next week. Maybe I didn't take a long enough break when she was born. I'm always exhausted. I took a sleeping pill last night, in fact, and shut the door of my room. She just won't sleep through the night; she's up every hour. The nanny goes home at the end of the day, so I'm left with the exhausting night-time schedule. And of course I worry that I'm not really a part of her everyday life. For me, my mix of emotions would best be described as exhausted, frustrated, confused and complex.

But I do believe women should be working. It is all very difficult because there is no easy answer. We have a lot to give the work environment. But maybe everyone should try ideally for a mixed portfolio. Being stuck on a career ladder, you can become jaded and boring. The pressures on working mothers can be unbearable. We need time to nurture our best qualities. And to have time for ourselves.

I think women should be giving a lot more thought to their competing guilts, the conflicting loyalties, and the way we desperately try to please everyone, *all* the time.

A European MP, Larraine, based in Brussels, is 36 years old with two children aged 9 and 4. And she works very, very hard. Yet Larraine never loses her guilt over not giving her children enough of her time. The children, she says, should be more, or at least just as, important as her work in politics.

To the surprise of those who know Larraine best, who watch her rushing around fitting in appointments, squeezing time for her children in the daily routine, this highly motivated and driven woman confesses that her fantasy would be to have given up work altogether until her children were 5 years old – and then to have returned only part time.

How can she make such a statement when one of her

major political programmes is to promote the need for more childcare and support for working mothers?

It's very difficult to know if I say this because I'm so removed from that way of life. But, really, it is my ideal fantasy. This is how I *feel* as a woman and a mother. But I was brought up to stick at things, under the Protestant ethic. And deep down I know I enjoy all the work and being so involved.

I'm very committed and responsible as a politician, but I'm always trying to cut down my work hours. I get the children up in the mornings, we have breakfast together. I take the elder one to school and the younger one to nursery. Then I come to the office for the working day. I'm exhausted *all* the time, and the consequence tends to be that I shout at my husband. I tell him we can see each other when the children are grown up!

I'm pulled three ways: by work, home and husband. He's not at all happy about putting off the time for *us* for fifteen years.

The trouble for me is that often I feel a failure as a mother and a failure at work. But maybe that's just part of the human condition. When I'm with the children, for instance, I notice the difference during the holidays when I have an extended amount of time with them. They're not so desperate for my attention then. Work days, when I come home around 5 p.m., they're flying at me, jumping all over me. I do feel children need as much of your time as they can get. My husband says I'm being overdramatic and that my worrying is all to do with my angst. So I give them as much as I can.

Larraine also demonstrates how the female guilt-quotient can come into play, despite the obvious importance of her work. When her younger child was suddenly taken very ill a year ago, she rushed straight to the hospital as soon as she received the phone call and didn't leave her bedside for three weeks.

I didn't think to tell anyone at work, or rearrange my workload in advance. And, the strange thing was, no one seemed to have noticed I'd been gone. Except for their concern about my child, they might just have ignored me.

In that sense, I'm now sure that a lot of the guilt we feel towards work may be self-induced. I disinvolved myself totally from the world of politics for that time. I didn't phone in to say I wouldn't be there to vote. One of the doctors finally reminded me of my responsibilities. I was shocked to hear him saying it – that I should return to work. My daughter's life was *far* more important. My husband, however, kept on working right through the crisis. That must be the male way of dealing with such severe problems.

NEEDING TO KEEP CONTROL

Most women, who have achieved any level of success at work, know that they have had to be twice as good as the average man to reach that position. There is a strong streak of perfectionism running through such women. When they become mothers, says a noted American psychiatrist, Dr Elisabeth Herz, from the George Washington University Medical Center, in Washington DC, there is a tendency to inflict their own overly high expectations on themselves – not just as professionals but as mothers.

But, when we have a child, it is impossible to impose that same kind of control on the infant or on our relationship with the child. They are a law unto themselves – often at our expense.

> Women very often imagine that their career will continue as before, and at the same time they will be a perfect mother [says Dr Herz]. But it is all a myth. Either your career has to go into second place for a time, or maybe it's just a question of accepting that you will not be shooting up the academic ladder and writing ten major articles a year. Somehow, the mother has to decide that she will pay for the best possible nanny, and that she will *not* be fully available to her child – if she is to continue with her career.

It is most important not to set high expectations that cannot be fulfilled, because you will then create unhappiness in your profession and unhappiness at home.

The career woman, Dr Herz points out, may realistically have had less contact with children than other women –

before motherhood. She will probably have been studying and working hard, and maybe did not know other people with young children. Looking after an infant can be a terrifying prospect. But, because of her achieved competence in her work, she finds it especially frustrating now to find herself incompetent.

Frustration and irritation might lead to anger at her husband, or at herself (which will emerge as depression). It's very useful to admit the likelihood that you won't be a 'perfect mother' from the start, and to recognise you are going to have to learn everything. Don't make any assumptions. Motherhood is not something you take on and can fit in easily between board meetings.

Dr Herz comments:

> I know that all the 'superwoman' myths, with the picture of the elegant, trim, marvellously dressed executive going out to work and coming home to play happily with her baby, has left the 'real' woman feeling very inadequate. She is constantly comparing herself with others. And constantly falling short of what others appear able to do. In America, particularly, what we are experiencing now is the feeling that to be a failure is one of the most devastating things that can happen!

CHILDCARE – MAYBE THE NUMBER ONE STRESSOR

Finding the loving nanny, housekeeper, babysitter, childminder or nursery place – the working mother's first prerogative – may well become the biggest stressor in her life. We've all heard the horror stories. And if a new working mother is trying to steel up her nerves, confront her guilt, they don't fall too well on her ears. But, there is no way around this; some women have gone through the most awful experiences.

For all the women who tell you that their nanny is the most important and lovable person in the world, that one nanny has been with the family for five years, that she could never have coped without her, etc., you'll easily find another woman for whom the very issue of childcare has become the thorniest problem in her life.

One woman I met told of coming home from work to find an empty house. Her au pair had just taken off, left the house for good – leaving the children at school. Fortunately, they had been taken to a friend's house. 'It was the biggest nightmare a mother could imagine,' says the mother. And she never again trusted an au pair.

Some other working mothers will hint darkly that these sorts of problems are probably indicative of the woman's deep down ambivalence about working or continuing her career. However, it has to be said that there are people who have more difficulties than others in finding good childcare (mother substitutes) because they are choosier than others. Maybe they are greater perfectionists; maybe they are more insecure about their role as a mother; maybe they are less able at managing an employee, at delegating responsibility; or maybe it all just depends on sheer luck.

Certain areas have a greater abundance of young or mature women available, willing and suitable for this type of work. Working mothers in rural areas have expressed more problems in finding live-in childcare, as the young women usually available for nannying prefer to live in major cities. As for nurseries, which many women would find a more amenable alternative to that of handing over their baby to a 'substitute mother' – there are notoriously few such healthy, well-run and affordable environments in the nation at this time.

IS OUR TRUST IN THIS PERSON JUSTIFIED?

Such is the desire for those committed to their career, or deeply in need of returning to work, to believe in the 'substitute mother' we have found; such is the level of despair or panic felt when one leaves abruptly, thereby forcing either mother or father to face time off work, that we all have a tendency to jump at the most likely looking person and believe

in her absolutely. With luck that faith is justifiable. Sometimes
it is not.

Megan, a 44-year-old manager with a large national
company, mother of a 2-year-old daughter, has now managed
to negotiate a job-share with her company – and at the same
time a place in a nursery set up for career mothers. She was
forced into this change in attitude towards her work after a
disappointing experience with a daily nanny when originally
she returned full-time to work:

> I found the relationship with the nanny very hard. She seemed to
> be taking over from me. We resented each other, I think, in
> different ways. I'm sure she was very good with my daughter, but
> I'd come home and the house would be a shambles. I'd run
> around cleaning up and I was beginning to think 'She's having all
> the good times with Suzy and I get to do all the boring work'. It
> was as though I was still the 'wife' in a bizarre way.
>
> Yet I'm in a very senior management position at work and am
> used to dealing with people. If I were doing it again, I would be
> tighter with her, as I am with the people who work for me in the
> office. You just feel so vulnerable when you're dealing with a
> nanny, because this person is looking after your child. I couldn't
> upset her in any way. Also I worried because she was not
> supervised at all. I would dearly have loved to sneak back home,
> to spy on her!
>
> The crunch came when I got home one evening at 6.30 p.m.
> and they weren't there. She hadn't phoned or asked my per-
> mission to keep my daughter out so late. In the end they came
> back around 7 p.m. – but by then I was crazy with worry. She'd
> gone round to a friend's house and had 'not noticed the time'.
>
> The nursery has been so much better. I'm very appreciative of
> how lucky I've been to find the place. In fact, I sometimes wonder
> whether if the nursery had been there, I might have stayed on at
> work full time. Maybe I wouldn't have become such a victim to
> stress as I was.

For Helene, 36, a highly enterprising woman who runs her
own company in a small city, who is mother of 8- and 5-year-
olds, the lack of suitable people for childcare has proved her
biggest problem:

There just are not the type of people around here who I would want to leave my children with. When they were little, I worked from home doing a variety of jobs. Since setting up this company, though, I have to work long hours. I cannot be there to pick them up from school or to take them to after-school activities. Nor do I have time for housework.

The only people qualified for this type of work are the fully trained nannies who only want to work with babies. Otherwise, I'm afraid we're left with the non-starters. Being such a busy person myself, working so hard, I get annoyed and frustrated at the lack of standards and sloppy ways. It's a permanent headache for me.

THE SINGLE WORKING MOTHER: HOW EASILY THE SYSTEM CAN FAULT

Helene admits that much of her stress, and the constant feeling of fatigue, is probably associated with the fact she is divorced. As a single working parent, her life seems to have narrowed down to two elements: work and looking after her children. For Helene there is no social life, no one to share the problems with, and no support that she doesn't pay for either.

Sue, a solicitor in a big London firm, is a 43-year-old single mother with a 9-year-old son. Sue is a gentle, soft-spoken woman who seems to radiate a delightful aura of motherliness. Yet, in her own description, she is a 'worn-out wreck'. Now well paid, with an established place in the firm, she recognises that in many ways her position is one of privilege. Although a single parent from the time of her son's birth, she has been able to survive. Now she owns a lovely home, enjoys a certain status in her job, and has even managed to establish a relationship for her son with his father that they both enjoy.

I'd always thought we would eventually marry, but now I realise I was fooling myself plus, of course, he was deceiving me. I'd also got it into my head that I would never be able to have children, after a major ovarian operation when I was 23.

I went along to the clinic for a pregnancy test, feeling a

complete fraud. When it was positive, I was overjoyed. But this was nearly ten years ago, and my position at work was not at all secure. I felt very vulnerable. I was new in the firm, and surrounded by male colleagues who all seemed to have nice wives and homes in the country, with neat children being looked after by their highly educated mothers. As far as they knew, I didn't even have an official 'boyfriend'. The father of my child could not make the commitment either to marry or live with me. So I'd never talked about him at work.

Lawyers are a very chauvinistic lot. Women in the legal profession get to know that very fast. I had to keep my head well down. I was off work longer than I intended because I had a lot of physical problems during the pregnancy. But once I returned to work – and I was so unrealistic I only rushed around and found a childminder the weekend before – I just worked. I arranged my hours to finish by 5 p.m. – because that's what the childminder demanded. She was really tough!

I suppose I could have changed minders, but I never gave it any thought. When you're caught on the treadmill of work, and worrying about your child, you don't indulge in the luxury of thinking, 'I'll shop around for a new childminder.' You're just grateful as each day passes without calamity! Every day, I'd rush out at 5 p.m. and have a nightmare drive to the minder's. If I was a minute late, she'd tell me off.

I guessed what my male colleagues were saying about me. But I made myself cut those comments out of my mind. And I stuck to my regime. I was just never around for evening meetings or drinks, either for business or pleasure. I haven't done anything like that for nearly the past ten years.

It's felt as though I've dotted and carried one for all those years. In time my son went to nursery and then school, but there were still frequent problems with sickness and holidays, and so on. It's been a constant hassle and strain.

The point I'm at now is that my child is getting older. I've kept up my job. I've kept the show on the road. Things are no longer so frantic all the time. And I'm giving myself permission to say, 'I can't stand this way of living!' Really, most of the time it's a matter of just keeping going: job, self, child, home. There's no real quality of life, no real time to relax. And certainly no time to make a new relationship. If you're a single mother, with a full-time job, it seems you end up with no time at all for yourself.

So I'm beginning to wonder whether there could be another way. Could I leave the security, the salary, the pension? I've got some brain left, I think – could I use it to live a happier, easier life? I'd love to devote some time to something I really want to do even though I may find it doesn't work out in the end. Who knows, maybe I'd miss the structures, the rat race, the tearing home at the end of the day!

But that's not to say all single mothers find the going so tough. Dee, now 31, mother of a 2-year-old son, and in a new position of junior management with a fairly small publishing company, has found the going reasonable – except for lack of sleep:

I didn't expect to be a 'single parent', as such. I was 28 when I conceived and I was fortunate to be at a stage in my career when I could negotiate an acceptable maternity leave arrangement. When I came back to work full time, I was specific about the hours, 9 a.m.–5 p.m., because my childcare arrangements were 8.30 a.m.–5.30 p.m. Then, when I was offered my current job, I was equally explicit, although I did say that with twenty-four hours' notice I could make arrangements to work late.

For the past six months, I have been able to reduce my working week to four days in the office (with a concurrent loss of one-fifth pay and holiday entitlement). This is an open-ended arrangement and I can return full time when I want.

In some ways, it's probably easier doing all this as a single parent. I can make plans to benefit just the *two* of us: my son and myself. It is imperative for both our emotional well-beings that I have the contrast between work and domestic life, as it obviates any resentment I might harbour at feeling trapped. For a variety of reasons – emotional, practical and financial – it's essential that I work. And I do feel fortunate that I am able both to parent and to work with considerable enjoyment.

However, nothing could have prepared me for what motherhood was/is like. Nothing can reveal the sheer joy of seeing your child at the end of a day, or the sheer desperation of trying to function on two hours' sleep! Motherhood summons up emotions, resources, reserves of stamina and endurance you don't know exist. My only real dream in life now is to have a full night's sleep ... And somehow to achieve a position where I could have another child or children.

But that would depend on a lot of things ... I'd keep on working in some way, however, with or without husband and a larger family. I recognise the need in me for that.

AN EVERYDAY STORY OF NEVER-ENDING CONFLICTS

Annette, 37-year-old consultant therapist with a senior position in a psychiatric clinic, mother of 12- and 8-year-old boys, describes the conflicts that run through any woman's life when she is involved with the juggling act that characterises career/motherhood.

Sometimes Annette feels the compromises are too strongly against her. But she would not be prepared to devote herself full time to career, and consequently part time to the boys' welfare. So the compromise rests with part-time career and part-time motherhood:

Where I work it is rather unusual in being very tolerant of women with children. It's possible here to do a job-share or to work part time. You'll see the car park emptying out at 3 p.m. as we scurry off to pick our children up from school. I plan my timetables with the heavy work in the mornings. Then maybe I give lectures or see clients in the early afternoons. After 3 p.m., it's tennis lessons and football – the boys' schedule. And at night I might work late on a paper I have to give the next morning.

My husband doesn't have to do all that. I still feel that women's advocates have addressed only the physical issues of motherhood, and not the emotional pressures. What about the effect of the guilt? Even if better childcare were available, we'd still feel the pressures within. It's a question of how we handle the conflicts.

Career-wise, I feel I'm terrifically ambitious and creative. I suppose we women have to try to give up the omnipotent part that wants to be everywhere, doing everything. I'm an immediate and impatient type of person. And I *want* it all. But I'm just not prepared to hand over my children to someone else totally. You see what I mean? It is an ongoing conflict – with myself.

To get any further in my career, I would have to be prepared to back out of my children's life. And who's to say that another

person would bring them up properly? Or that they w
loved and secure that way?

YOUR PERSONAL STRESS QUOTIENT

When I filled in a questionnaire in a popular women's
magazine, a couple of years ago, I was shocked to discover in
the simple listing of Yes and No, that I was running very close
to burn-out level myself. My adaptability and survivability
were tremendous (which is why I hadn't noticed anything very
wrong!). But although I was struggling on, working, caring
for children, trying to run a home – there were vital com-
ponents missing.

I'd had a quiet nagging feeling that no one really cared, or
took notice of, what I was so busy struggling with. But it took
lists of questions to bring the real truth home to me.

Aware now how important such a basic questionnaire can
be – the simple reminder of home truths that we don't think
appear threatening – I have devised my own self-scoring
checklist that any working mother can fill in.

There are times, in all our lives, when we need to stand back
and view ourselves objectively. None of us wants to be
trapped, scurrying like rabbits between endless holes in the
ground – desperately fighting for mere survival or to prove
ourselves capable. This is one way of catching a sense of your
own private emotional barometer. As Sue, the solicitor, earlier
in this chapter, reminded us: the quality of *our* lives is just as
important as parenting, or career. We count too!

The best way to score from this questionnaire, rather than
giving yourself numbers, is to highlight the questions that
mean something to you. Then read it back as though it were
an essay on your current life and emotional state.

1. *The very obvious major stressors* in life, often discounted
as *too* obvious
At work, for example, have you changed your job or
employer; been promoted or demoted; moved work location;

been fired or resigned? Have you had to take on new responsibilities at work? Have you been passed over for promotion? Or, do you feel that you might have been passed over?

2. What is the style of your working life?

Do you have a long journey to and from work? Are the hours convenient to your family pressures? Is the place you work in friendly and welcoming or bleak and depressing? Is your work interesting and varied? Or full of boring tasks? Does your work bring you positive satisfaction that outweighs any negative feelings? Do you feel in control of your working environment? Or are you at the mercy of an unsympathetic supervisor or boss? Do you have responsibility for others at work? Do you like your work? Is there enough room for your own creativity? Does your work life introduce you to enough other people? Are these contacts social as well as work oriented? Are your colleagues largely a source of pleasure or irritation?

3. Personal stressors that have recently affected your life

Have you recently moved house or town? Have you experienced bereavement of a close family member or friend? Has there been any particular severe problem with a close family member or friend? Have you, or a close family member, recently been separated or divorced? Have you entered a new relationship? Or recently found yourself without any close, intimate, relationship? Have you suffered illness or injuries in recent times? Has your family size recently grown – a new baby, adoption, or other person coming to live with you? Have there been any major financial changes – loss of savings, loss of partner's job, etc.? Have you undergone crime, theft, an accident, or similar major trauma?

4. What about pressures in your private life?

Do you and your husband/partner get along well and smoothly? Are there conflicts over household tasks? Or over childcare? Can you talk to your husband/partner about ways to change the situation? If you cannot talk to him, do you know why? Or is there anything you can do, without too much trauma, to improve the situation for *you*? Do you have any serious money problems or debts that are worrying you? Are you having serious problems with a child, or with another family member? Do you feel that work, family, or the question of how you share your time, are real problems?

5. *And pressures from those around you?*
Do the people closest to you make time for you, when *you* are in need? Does your partner and/or children understand when you are upset or feeling vulnerable? Do you feel loved by your family and friends? Is your sexual relationship with husband/ partner a source of pleasure or conflict? Do you feel the time you are spending with your family, outside work, is 'quality time'? Do you feel important and needed to your family members? Do you have good close friendships with people outside of your family?

6. *How good are you at seeking support?*
Do you seek help when difficulties arise? Or worry about them alone? Do you know who to turn to, for talking over problems at work or at home? Do you willingly seek advice and/or support? Would you seek help from a doctor or counsellor for personal problems? Or do you feel you should be able to handle everything yourself? Can you discuss with your boss or supervisor if you feel the workload is becoming intolerable, or you have extra problems at home?

7. *How good are you at handling your situation?*
Do you take time out for yourself in your busy schedule? Are there hobbies or outside interests that take your mind off work and/or family? Are you able to put aside certain worries as not too important? Do you make time for exercise, or for some relaxing occupation? Do you bolt your food and feel mealtimes are just another job? Would you force yourself to finish a project, or meet a deadline, even if you were exhausted? Are you a driven and competitive person by nature? Do you mostly put others' needs before your own? Do

you have a sense of humour? Or has that got lost in recent years? Do you give yourself rewards, for a job well done?

8. *How good are you at handling time?*

Can you set aside tasks that are not too important? Do you find you complete one project before moving on to another? Or are you constantly distracted from finishing things? Do others dump work or responsibilities on you? Are you always so busy doing for others, that you fail to get your own work, or projects, done? When it comes down to the conflict between work and family, do you allocate your time efficiently – and to the best possible advantage? Can you think of ways better to divide up your time?

4   PART OF A LIFETIME'S PLAN

Jane, the building society manager, just 32 years old, is about to return to work after sixteen weeks of maternity leave. Although her company had scant, if any, provision for a female executive to be taking such leave, this pregnancy nevertheless fits within her overall vision of life:

> I've been married all my working life – so I've been lucky in always having a steady relationship, which I think helps with your credibility within an industry like the building societies. I knew that I did not want to hit 40 and not have children, so by the time I was 31 we thought we'd try and see what would happen. Well, it all happened straight away, which was something of a shock, as I imagined it would take some time – in itself that was meant to help me adjust to this major life change.
>
> Up until the moment of conception, I had always played the career game – as you have to. I'd avoided the question of whether I would ever have children, in interviews, and in general chat around the office. If you let it be known that you want kids it would be a black mark against you. My company is positive towards its women employees in many ways. I've had no problems in terms of promotions. In fact, I would say that my movement up the career ladder has been rapid; better than that of some of my male colleagues. But if companies want to keep good female employees they will need different guidelines in the future for working mothers.

Jane is typical of today's young women: she grew up *expecting* to blend work with motherhood, and nothing so far has taken her off track:

> Friends told me I'd feel differently once I became a mother, but that hasn't happened so far. I've enjoyed spending these weeks at

home with my baby; but really just me and this little baby, alone in our house, it's not enough. I'm not using my other mental capacities.

WHEN TO FIT PREGNANCY IN WITH A CAREER PLAN

For Kathy, now 37, mother of a 7-year-old boy, also a manager within the building society industry (but not in quite such a senior position as Jane), the pregnancy was meant to fit into a major career plan. But problems at work forced a decision to have the baby earlier than she'd originally imagined. Looking back, she is not sure if the timing was quite right. Kathy had had no intentions of having a baby as early as age 30 – hoping to be further up the career ladder before she made such a move:

> However, due to contraction in the industry seven years ago, promotion was not as rapid as I'd hoped for. We decided to go ahead with the pregnancy then, as the job I held at that time was not very demanding. We felt this would make the whole process easier to cope with. The plan only really came together when my husband and I sat down and looked at what we wanted for the future. We decided then to move away from the big city – so we could buy a house and where we also believed there'd be more chance for better jobs than in the heavily competitive city world.
>
> We probably should have made that move earlier as both of us have now benefited career-wise from it. I've had three promotions in four years, whereas in the other job I stayed in one position for five years.
>
> I sussed out fairly early on what I'd really like to do, and what I would let myself do, relative to the family unit. Ideally I'd like to go on and study for an MBA [Master of Business Administration], but I won't take that time until my son is perhaps a student himself. Also, although both my husband and I would probably benefit now from a move back to the city for better promotion, I wouldn't do that to my son. It's hard enough fitting work hours into the day and giving him enough time, without adding on the extra burden of commuting and those very long hours.

STAYING IN THE CITY MADE LIFE EASIER FOR SOME

Unable to make the actual decision – when is the best time to have a baby – some women find themselves arranging their lives, subconsciously readying themselves for parenthood. Sarah, the now disillusioned senior manager in accountancy with a multinational oil company, never sat down and planned it this way but the unspoken terms were that if they began a family she would continue working.

When Sarah graduated from university, she knew that she wanted to succeed in the male world. To that end, she told the careers' adviser not to suggest any 'female'-type professions to her.

But children were always in the back of her mind, and now she is sure their decision, when she married at age 25, to buy a house large enough for a family, close to the city centre, in an area that would give them space for a live-in nanny and a couple of kids, plus ease of getting to and from work, was dictated by that inner force:

> I became more serious about family in my early 30s. But then it did take a couple of years for the system to work, and now we have a son and a daughter aged 5 and 2 years. My own problem with fitting motherhood into my career was in not understanding well enough how the corporate system works – making a developmental move when I was pregnant meant that I slipped out of the system very badly. I was naive and innocent then, and imagined they'd support me. I've certainly learned my lesson!

PANIC SETS IN AS YOU HIT YOUR LATE 20s AND EARLY 30s

The women whose families were already well set up before they embarked seriously on career have very different views on this type of question. Linda, the director of a PR company, was a twice-divorced single mother of two daughters when she found that hunger for bread on the table made her focus her attentions on career. Anne, in sales management with a major computer firm, was divorced from her first marriage, with no children, when she realised she was a total misfit – an unmarketable woman, of near 30, who had never held down a 'paying' job. That realisation set her on a determined path to catch up with the sort of position being enjoyed by her peers.

But for women hitting their late 20s or early 30s, the question is most pressing. Should they be having children now while their bodies are still young enough? Should they wait until their career is better established?

Gillian, one of the co-founders of a wealthy and busy company, was 34 when she had her now 3-year-old daughter:

> Everyone knew I wanted a child when I married. Within about six months I was pregnant. But I can't fool you by saying they haven't been tough years. Right now, I couldn't face being pregnant again, much as I'd love a second child, because there just isn't room for so much work and children.
>
> Don't get pregnant in your mid-30s is my advice. That's the time to prove yourself at work. Wait till you're over 35 and an executive; that's the time to have kids. Really, women can't do both well. You cannot put a big push in your career, and run a home and marriage.

OLDER MOTHERS

When I was facing the prospect of my first pregnancy at age 31, I considered myself an 'older mother'. Doctors then called anyone over 30, having their first child, an elderly *prima gravida*. But times have changed and I doubt if many women would use the term unless they had passed 37–40 years.

Women come to motherhood these days at such ripe 'old' ages for a variety of reasons: because of second marriages, late marriages, undecided feelings, concentration on career, or infertility. Very often older mothers will speak of their children in terms of God-given blessings. They may indeed also find their adjustment is easier because, as Gillian points out, financial and career-position are in a state of mature stability.

On the minus side, however, no older mother can discuss her changed life without using such terms as 'exhaustion' or 'fatigue'. Most mention their fears about having a healthy baby; their worries that either they or their husbands might not be around by the time their child is a young adult. In the long run, no one is likely to offer the definitive advice that women should wait till their mid to late 30s before beginning a family. Yet we cannot overlook that later motherhood does certainly have its pluses.

WOMEN DOCTORS – LATER MOTHERS

Interestingly, women doctors figure quite highly in the statistics of later motherhood. The strenuousness of their training, and impossibility of 'fitting' pregnancy in with their early years as working women, seem to account for this. Ruth, now 41, a senior medical officer in local government, is the mother of a 14-month-old son.

Ruth had been infertile for most of her married life though, as both she and her husband shared an ambivalence about having children, they had done little about trying to conceive until recent years:

I discovered then you can plan as much as you like – to fit motherhood in with a career structure – but things may just not go according to plan if you fail to conceive.

Ideally, I'd originally envisaged having children early on in my career. I was already married as a medical student, which is quite unusual in itself. In fact, it would have been impossible to continue as a hospital doctor if I had become a mother at that time. When I was doing registrar jobs, on rota, living-in one night in five, on call two or three nights in a row, and not on the type of salary I am now, it would have been hopeless. We would not have been able to afford a live-in nanny. Most probably I'd have given up or gone part time which so many women are forced to do.

By the time I took this position in the civil service, my hours as an administrator became much more reasonable. My husband had gone off the idea of having children when we were younger and I had concentrated on my career instead. But then I really began to feel the need for a baby. As I was getting older, any idea of planning the pregnancy soon disappeared. I had some tests done to see why we weren't conceiving, and then the plan was to get pregnant and hang the career!

No one could be happier to have a child now. But still it's a long day, as we live an hour away from my place of work. I leave the house at 8 a.m. and half kill myself to get home for 6.30–6.45 p.m. At least in the civil service the hours are more informal than they ever would be in a hospital. Workwise it has been very straightforward for me. I was able to take eight months off – they're so generous here. And no one, for a minute, thought I wouldn't come back! The Chief Medical Officer was the first person I told. Knowing my age, I think he was quite a gentleman about it. He just blinked, expressed his delight, and said, 'You will be coming back, won't you?'

Christine, also a woman doctor, now aged 39, is consultant radiologist for a large city health area and mother to a 6-month-old daughter. She was even more tied up in work and career:

I had absolutely no maternal instinct and planned never to have a family. I was married at 23, and both my husband and I led full social and professional lives. Our careers were planned without any consideration of family at all.

However, at 37, I suddenly felt I might regret having no children. I was also worried I might not be fertile after nineteen years of unbroken contraception. Much to my surprise, however, I became pregnant immediately, and then had very mixed feelings – so much so I concealed the pregnancy until I was five months, by which time it was blatantly obvious. But I still ignored the pregnancy, by working to the week before the baby was born – by elective C-section.

At the time I became pregnant, I was in charge of X-ray studies for the whole health district and I was on endless committees. I knew I did not want to slip into middle age on an endless tide of committee and professional work. But I didn't want to relinquish the directorship of various departments either, so I returned to administrative work two weeks after the baby was born. And I resumed full-time work four weeks later.

My husband is a surgeon and can provide no domestic back-up or support with childcare even if he wanted to. I have a live-in nanny and a cleaning lady. And I'm lucky that our daughter sleeps well. I could not have had less maternal instinct – I still have no feeling for other people's children – yet we've both been amazed at our attitude to parenthood and to our daughter. We're both *delighted* to have become parents at this late stage.

It really is so much easier to reach the top of the tree and have a family when you're emotionally, financially and in every other way stable, than it would be if you were trying to struggle your way up the ladder.

THE PATCHWORK CAREER: A FEMALE 'NORM'

But for so many women, in the past, and the situation continues today, careers are not begun at age 23 to be pursued with vigour, determination and a non-negotiable five-year plan – taking motherhood in along the way – until retirement. So many women put their own careers in a second-best position, or holding pattern, to fit in with a husband's plans and ambitions. They may travel and take the family along, to follow his work to the ends of the earth. They may stop for a few years and restart once the young family is settled. They may move in and out of full-time and part-time work. Many of these women's stories quite naturally appear in the chapter devoted to that topic of part-time or self-employed work, or those who run their own businesses. Many, indeed, have been very successful following non-traditional lines of work. Others feel the 'quality' of the balance they have achieved, between work and family commitments, is justification in itself.

But now, I would like to broaden out the discussion of how motherhood fits into women's lifetime plans by looking at the sort of chequered careers so many of us find ourselves drawing on our own multi-coloured portrait of life.

FORCED INTO TAKING HER CAREER PART TIME

By comparison with Christine, women doctors a decade or so ago had nothing like the ease of choice and decision-making available to them once they became pregnant. There simply was no maternity leave or support. If you wanted to continue working as a doctor while you had young children, you made your own provisions – and tried to fit them around your husband's and colleagues' prejudices. Surprisingly, a number of women did just that. Medicine was one of those careers that attracted women's loyalty long before legal supports came to help them.

Deirdre, aged 58, a hardworking former GP, and now consultant psychiatrist in a large hospital outside London, is a strikingly attractive woman who has raised and sent six children off to university – as well as juggling her own career demands. Reflecting on the difficulties for her generation, she explains:

> I have been married for nearly thirty-five years to another doctor. I worked full time for a couple of years before the first child was born. Then three more children followed during which years I worked part time, and intermittently for six more years, until I became a full-time GP. Then there were two more children and I began retraining in psychiatry.

Six years ago, Deirdre achieved consultant status – and has carved out quite an international reputation within her field of women's psychiatry. There has been, she points out, very little support along the way:

> All my pregnancies were planned, but looking back it was a mistake to have four children within three years, as I didn't enjoy their babyhood as much as I would have liked. I also experienced some resentment at having to work full time when the fourth one was only 9 months old, as my husband was then earning very little. But I resented it even more that I had to give up that position when his income increased.
>
> In those days, maternity leave was just not possible. I always knew it would be difficult. And I am envious of the present-day working mothers for their rights regarding maternity leave, and the support expected and given them by their spouses.

YOU NEED A SKILLS' INVENTORY

Joanna Foster, chairman of the Equal Opportunities Commission (EOC), finds her interest in issues of women's equality at work – and the availability of childcare – is fired by her own background:

'Everything I do, all the issues I now support, are because of my own experience,' she emphasises. Formerly head of the Pepperell Unit of the Industrial Society, a body which encourages women returnees, she has long been active in providing help to motivate women up the management ladder. Joanna herself is a married woman, of 48, with two teenage children – her career exemplifies how masterfully women can and do adapt themselves, against all the odds.

As her husband's career has been in the international field of business management, the Fosters have always travelled. Joanna took the two young children around the world with them:

I left school with two A levels, knowing only that I wanted to do 'something with people'. I've developed areas in myself out of necessity – language skills, editing a newspaper, running nursery schools.

We lived first in Paris and then moved to Pittsburgh, in the USA, where I wasn't allowed to work because I had no work permit. So, on my fortieth birthday, I embarked on a degree in psychology.

She became involved with the psychiatric unit at the University of Pittsburgh and worked on research into stress management. Joanna's particular interest was in the problems of relocation and its effect on families:

Many women are in stop/start careers. What we need is a skills' inventory. Rather than saying 'I've only been at home', we need advice on how to explain the talents learned along the way. Each piece of the patchwork is valid – towards a full description of the person.

The Fosters resettled in Oxford, but two years later her husband was offered a position back in Paris. This time Joanna refused to uproot the family. Instead her husband commuted weekly.

Research shows that 36 per cent of the workforce are 'inner-directed' workers, motivated less by security and money than by a need for personal growth:

> Many women fall into this category. They feel the need for a balance between work and family life. But men are also beginning to follow suit. Men are saying, 'There must be more to life than this'. The linear career pattern of most men is altering. One school of thought now says we'll all have to change our skills at least four times before the end of the century.

WHERE GIRLHOOD DREAMS ARE LOST

Women who have found work in medical, sociological, creative or even educational fields have often found their careers are transportable. When a husband's or family's needs dictate, they pick up the collective baggage and move themselves. Not all manage to carve out professional, recognised, or high-status careers along the way. But most struggle on, strangely content with 'some' career rather than no career at all.

Annie, a 34-year-old with two children aged 10 and 12, never quite carved out the sort of career she had once dreamed of:

> I wanted to do medicine but my brother was awarded a medical scholarship and, despite my better grades, I was offered a teacher's scholarship. I left university because I just didn't like the work. Then I was married at 19, after completing a secretarial course. We went off to travel and I became pregnant – unplanned. The second baby came three years later, also unplanned.
>
> I have always worked, except during the last stages of pregnancy and the first months after the baby is born. However, I have done certain jobs to fit in – so that the children were cared for

either by my husband or myself. I waitressed and managed restaurants at nights and cared for the children during the day. Since they have been at school, I have gone back to secretarial work. Partly it is for financial reasons, but also because I feel the need to get out and do something. I'm fairly happy with my ability as a mother and a worker. What has suffered is my ability to be a good marriage partner.

There is great satisfaction in being back in the 'outside' world and particularly from being with different women – some of whom are mothers like me. We behave differently at work, and I find that contact very satisfying. Also I'm earning enough to allow my husband to give up his hated career and become an actor.

HOW CAN WE KNOW WHAT LIFE PLAN WILL FIT US BEST?

Just how and why we make the decision to juggle a patchwork career, or continue on determinedly through the male-defined full-time career (with the very obvious rewards of security, privileges and outside recognition) is the trickiest question to answer. Quite often women seem to let the major life decisions be made for them. Are we not programmed to be so passive from early days? Two stories of women who have pursued very different career paths – with differing attitudes to the balance of work/family life – finish off the story.

NANCY: UNIVERSITY LECTURER AND THERAPIST

Nancy has just turned 40, her three sons are aged 10, 8 and 6. Her husband is a doctor. They live well. Maybe Nancy doesn't really need to work. But she continues juggling her family's demands, and her own inner needs – to be there as 'housewife, wife and mother' – at the same time as struggling to carve out a career niche for herself.

To be honest, I just adopted my mother's lifestyle at first – that I'd want to be at home taking care of my babies and then, maybe ten years later, I'd return to work. But I realised pretty quickly that much as I loved them, I had to fulfil those other needs. I surprised myself, however, with my need to be working. As I look back it was difficult to work out then what it was I wanted.

When I was at home with the young children, I had a profound feeling of loneliness and missed friends and colleagues. My husband had just taken up a very responsible job with a hospital in a rural town – where I knew no one and people seemed very cliquy. In the end, I knew I had to get back to my work. I found a sitter and returned to finishing my MA. Then I began teaching at a local college – on a part-time basis. I also taught childbirth classes in the evenings and relaxation classes to other mothers.

Now I'm actually working full time – but not in the traditional sense. I do different things to fit in with my responsibilities to the children. I'm up at 5 a.m. – so I get my hour of quiet to take a shower and to think for myself. It's one of my favourite times of the day. I do the laundry and maybe make a casserole for dinner. Then I pack their school lunches, organise their shirts and sports clothes. Or sometimes I do a little bit of work. The boys go off to school and I go to my new office, at the college, arriving there at 8.30 a.m. I am acutely aware of the time pressure, as everything must be done by 3.30 p.m. when I return home to the boys.

I seldom go out to lunch, not only because of time but because I have a need to be quiet, by myself, and not just chatter, chatter, chatter all day. After 3.30 p.m. I'm busy taking the boys to sports practice or whatever. I take things along in the car to read while I wait. I like to cook, so I don't mind making the casseroles ahead of time. But I don't do the tablecloth-and-linen-napkins kind of meal. Also, as my husband is a hospital doctor he works very long hours, so I don't really think about his dinner. He just picks something up when he gets home. I don't wait up for him either!

After homework and reading time, it's getting on for 10 p.m., and I'm ready for bed myself. The main problem for me is that babysitters, or someone who can look after the boys during the holidays and after school, rule my life. I try to be home in the holidays, if I can. Now I'm looking forward to them being old enough to take care of themselves.

Sometimes I make a fuss about the inequities of the career patterns between my husband and myself. But I know I couldn't be the doctor, working those hours. Someone has to look after the children and the way I'm working seems to suit my life at the moment. Ultimately I'd like to return to university and complete my PhD.

Some days I feel very stressed – it's a real challenge doing a regular job, pursuing other interests such as the major conference I recently organised, trying to be a good mother, *and* a pleasant wife! I'd say I'm working harder now than I've ever worked in my life. I'm trying to do it all – and do it all *well*.

PHILIPPA: SUCCESSFUL HIGH-FLYER IN SENIOR MANAGEMENT WITH A MAJOR MULTINATIONAL COMPANY

Philippa, who is about to turn 40, is mother to three children, aged 9, 7 and nearly 2. She has been divorced, is now remarried and has recently started a new family. She holds one of the three top woman manager positions on the marketing side of a big company.

I was 30 when I had my first child, already well established in my career with this company which I joined on leaving university. I'd graduated with a chemistry degree. When I first began working, I imagined I'd soon be married and having children. In fact things didn't work out that way till ten years later.

With the first baby, I tried working from home because I couldn't afford a nanny at the time. Ten years ago women like me didn't think in those terms. In my business, working with computers, it was quite easy to work from home and to earn well. I cleared a lot of money, and managed to fit work into the evenings.

But it just wasn't the same as a career. I could not keep up the training. Although I felt guilty inside about it, I wasn't happy about being part time. I could see all those people overtaking me on the career ladder, so I told myself to face up to the facts. I'm an ambitious person and I wanted to get on. So I might as well go back full time. Whatever people say, part time is inadequate if you seriously want to succeed. It's just marking time.

I returned full time when my daughter was 6 months old. The company basically did the bare minimum for their women employees. To my horror, ten years later, by which time I was in senior management, I discovered they were equally unhelpful.

Two years later I was pregnant again. By this time I'd decided to transfer into marketing which is the only way to get ahead here. However, there were only one or two lady saleswomen out of a salesforce of more than 350, and I was five and a half months pregnant at the time, which was not the easiest situation!

But I had my son, hired a live-in nanny and went back to work full time when he was 5 weeks old. I became a saleswoman, and left my husband, all within the space of six months. Because it was I who was leaving the marriage, and the children were better off in the family home, I bought myself a flat.

My husband kept the children during the week and they came to me at weekends. The kind of work I do, and the hours involved, made it impractical for me to have them all week. In the computing world, when you're dealing with customers, it's very unpredictable. If the customer is having problems, you may have to go and sort it out, even if you're there all night. Also I travelled quite extensively.

At work my immediate colleagues were very supportive. I got the feeling they knew I'd messed up my marriage, and they just wanted to say, 'Don't screw up your career as well.' Then, five years ago, I met my new husband. We now have a son of just 2. I'm in a very high pressure situation at work, but my husband also works here, in a similar capacity, and we find we can work it all out very well. Whatever problems I have had with senior executives over my pregnancy and maternity leave, I've put behind me. You have to – to survive.

I've always been well organsed. We have a live-in nanny, a cleaner and someone to do the garden. If one of us works late, we can compare diaries and see who'll go home. Most of the time, one of us can get away to be home by 7 p.m. We try to balance it. Sometimes, I have had to say, 'Sorry, I must go home early', to my colleagues who are expecting me to stay.

I may not be the typical woman. When I get home about 7 p.m., I have a couple of hours of fun with my little boy and then he's off to bed. The older children still come for weekends, and we all take holidays together. It's perfect motherhood for me! I'm also in a well-paying position and have the privilege of being able to afford good help and support.

But now I'm pushing into an area where women haven't been before. I need to be free to pop over to Paris if I have to, or to go on courses, or to stay at meetings that drag on. For me, those compromises on my home life are fine.

5 PREGNANCY: A BOOST TO YOUR CAREER?

There's nothing quite like feeling sick and tired at work is there? Especially if you haven't yet dared reveal the truth of your pregnancy, either from personal fears that you may miscarry, or in trepidation of how your boss, or immediate colleagues, will react to the impending change in your personal, emotional and working life. As one woman so aptly remarked, 'We really need the time off at the beginning of pregnancy not at the end. It can be tough struggling on through the day when you're feeling lousy and just too tired to cope.'

Most women, however, are loath to take extra time off in those early months. Not only do they fear being castigated as an unreliable employee before motherhood itself has started; they recognise the need to save up any time off owing them until nearer the birth. There is often a feeling, too, of wanting to remain firmly in credit with the workplace.

Although women have been handling these situations for a couple of decades, there is surprisingly little information to help them deal with what can be a difficult nine months. This mother will certainly not be sitting at home knitting pink or blue bootees; nor will she be idly filling her days buying baby furniture and equipment. More likely she will be worrying about her expanding waistline and what clothes to wear to the office to disguise the all too obvious change in her life. She may be worrying whether she can take a nap at her desk, in privacy, when everyone disappears for lunch.

WHAT TO EXPECT OF THOSE NINE MONTHS

Women employees at British Petroleum (BP) recently gathered material and advice from other working mothers and compiled an excellent booklet based on what women can expect from pregnancy, their maternity leave and, ultimately, from the practice of working motherhood. The *Maternity Advice Pack* relates specifically to working conditions at BP and is excellent in discussing some of the emotional changes a woman may experience:

> If you think you may want children, the first thing to remember is that there is *no* truly convenient time. This applies equally to whether you want to continue working full time, part time or not at all.
>
> Nevertheless, there are a number of ways to make your life easier. There are no hard and fast rules – the best laid plans often come unstuck – and one of the first lessons one learns as a mother is that flexibility is a skill to be cultivated.

In another section, the writers (who are all working mothers themselves) warn that there is no way of guaranteeing yourself an easy ride through pregnancy:

> Some women sail through pregnancy with no problems at all, whereas others suffer to varying degrees from the 'usual minor ailments' associated with pregnancy.
>
> For a first-time mother, pregnancy is a new experience and it is impossible to predict how you will react to it. Your body goes through a number of significant changes, some of which may have an effect on your work. Pregnancy can be an emotional time for yourself and those close to you at home and at work. For those of you going through a second or subsequent pregnancy, you will have a fair idea of what to expect, but it is worth remembering that pregnancies can be very different.
>
> It is also worth remembering that it may be uncharted territory for your manager and colleagues. Your manager may never have had a pregnant woman among his or her staff, and may be unsure or unaware of the responsibilities. Your colleagues also may not have worked with a pregnant woman, and may be diffident.

They spell out that for women working within companies as complex as BP, it is up to the individual to find out:

(a) what has to be done about your job before your absence;
(b) what hand-over arrangement is needed for your stand-in or successor;
(c) what, if anything, you may be called upon to do during your absence;
(d) what needs to be done in the way of planning with management and personnel staff for your return.

As you will see in this and the following two chapters, the best laid plans can still go awry. You will be dealing with managers and colleagues who may have their own vested interests (or lack of interest) in pregnant women. You will be countering head on whatever disguised prejudices, or deeply felt emotions, the men or women surrounding you harbour towards women, mothers and children. Let us now look at how the women who participated in this book were treated during their pregnancies.

HANDLING WHAT YOU KNOW WILL BE A TRICKY SITUATION

Jane, the building society manager, described her situation at work once she had positive confirmation of the pregnancy which, if you recall, happened more quickly than she had imagined. There was her own element of shock at the impending changes to be overcome, as well as that of her colleagues:

> I didn't tell anyone for a while. Because of my age I wanted various tests done first, and also because of their perception of me at work I needed to bide my time and work out a strategy. I knew that I had a high profile and was known as career-oriented, and I was frightened of suddenly being written off as yet another 'pregnant woman'. I could imagine them saying, 'That'll be the end of Jane. She won't come back.'

In the end I sent a variety of personal notes to all my senior managers to let them know in *my way*. I didn't want them hearing the news on the grapevine, making their own judgements. This way I'd had a chance to think it all out before going public. I was very aware I'd be losing a certain amount of credibility in my position. These men knew only how their own wives had coped with motherhood; most of them, of course, have wives who stayed at home with young children. And that is the *only* pattern of experience they have. The best managers are those whose wives work – and have children. They, at least, understand.

YOUR IMMEDIATE SENIOR – MALE – CAN HAVE THE MOST IMPACT

Sarah, the accountant with a major company having her first baby at 33, faced a problem of confrontation with male senior management who did not sympathise with working mothers. Sarah had a very difficult time:

Now, in retrospect, I can see the cynicism many managers feel, because the numbers of senior women are few anyway and, in the past, many women who have said they would return to work in the end did not. It's a Catch-22 situation we women are caught in because it is not always easy to combine the two roles. I know of women in my company who changed their minds at the last minute – and they were probably instrumental in ruining the situation for me.

When I accepted that developmental move, which was supposed to be a career move, just before going on maternity leave, it had the effect of taking me out of the department where I was known and respected, away from my mentors and anyone who might be supportive, to new managers who weren't at all sympathetic of working mothers. I had no support behind me when I went off on maternity leave.

Even Judy, who works with an international banking house, where she continues to keep up the hours demanded in that type of world, found most of her colleagues were intrigued when she said she was planning to return to work:

People were quite solicitous; but apart from that they let me get on with it. A couple of colleagues, I could tell, didn't really expect me to return.

However, because my line of work is a consultancy, working on long-term projects, there was no need to hire a stand-in. The baby was my project for that six months. On my return, I discovered that no one had really picked up on all the loose ends I left behind. But at least they didn't need to replace me, *per se*, which helped me slot back in.

THE MANAGER REALLY COULDN'T BELIEVE HE WAS WORKING WITH A SALESWOMAN WHO WAS PREGNANT!

Philippa, one of three senior managers in the marketing division of a major computing company, wonders whether it was because of her attitude (she has never made any concessions at work to being a mother) that she has made it to the top. When she was pregnant for the third time, at age 38, in a much more senior and visible position, there were large and very threatening areas of confrontation to be coped with.

Once I had become a sales representative my career really began to take off. I was in a regional manager's position, in an area that was being badly hit by competition. My brief was a long-term strategy to improve things. It was a critical situation and highly visible within the company. The man in charge of the section is very sweet, but basically he could not come to terms with the fact that a woman can also be a serious businesswoman. So when I became pregnant there was definitely a problem. Here he was dealing with a woman in a crucial area, and she's pregnant!

I was put under a lot of pressure. He would try to sound very concerned, by saying 'Are you sure you can manage this?' I would remind him, 'It's my third baby. I know what I'm doing. I'm healthier than I've ever been in my life'. But still he maintained he was worried for me – that I was having a long drive at the time and that that was very stressful.

My career has always been very important to me. And I really

feared I was being put down, or eased out. In trying to be helpful
he was making things worse.

In the end, I compromised. Two months before the baby was
due I handed over the key job to my stand-in. As it happened, I
was whipped into hospital six weeks before the birth with
toxaemia, so I'd have had to leave anyway. But I know he was
putting pressure on me; his wife had never worked and he really
couldn't understand me. I discovered his real attitude when I
walked through the door on my first day back to work and he
said, 'Until I saw you here, I wasn't sure you'd actually come
back.'

MORE MEN LEAVE FOR CAREER ADVANCEMENT
THAN WOMEN DO TO HAVE BABIES

Anne, the 41-year-old mother of 5– and 2–year–olds, also a
senior manager in marketing with a computer firm, describes
her fear of announcing her second pregnancy:

Before I ever had children I was terrified of my company's
attitude. I remember once at an interview being asked, as I was
married, did I plan to have children and leave? I was furious at the
question and retorted that, in my experience, I'd seen more men
leaving, changing jobs for career advancement, than women
leaving to have babies.

But I kept quiet about the pregnancy until after three months
this second time, because by now I was on the sales staff. I had
miscarried before and I was expecting a certain amount of
hostility. I didn't protest too much about my condition, never
took a day off, and was determined to convince them that I was
serious about returning.

'It was as though I'd stabbed him in the back'

Ellen, now a director of a very successful design company,
well regarded among her colleagues, found that in her former
job – on the way up the career ladder – her boss 'acted as if I'd
stabbed him in the back' when she announced her pregnancy.
She was 31 years old and three months pregnant:

It was really a very male-oriented company. A lot of women were working there as designers but none of them dared to have babies. So it came as a shock all round. My boss actually referred to the pregnancy once as 'this awful thing you're doing'. I liked him a lot, and we're still good friends. So I was able to forgive him.

I had no deputies, no one I could hand my work over to. I knew they were dependent on my returning to work as soon as possible. Yet I wanted to spend six months with my baby. So I agreed to take no maternity leave, but for six weeks I would work from home. Then I began coming in for mornings only until the baby was 6 months old. Now, I see strong-minded women all round me saying, 'I'm taking 8 months off.' My own advice is to take as much time off as you can, or as you feel you need. It can be a killer trying to work to deadlines and cope with the baby. Your mind just doesn't work very well.

When I had the second baby, two and a half years later, I completely underestimated my colleagues again. They went into an absolute panic. Again I had worked out an arrangement whereby I could do a lot of the work from home. But in one meeting, my boss said in a very tense voice, 'Give me *exact* details of the hours you'll be working in the office.' I wasn't threatened by his behaviour. He's the nicest man, and I knew he was just worried that we'd never keep up with the workload. I said, 'Don't panic. Relax. I've planned it out carefully, it's all here on paper.' Then I wrote him a letter after that pointing out how brave I was, that I never moan about how hard it can be!

But I am determined in my work. I played down the pregnancies and never asked for any sympathy. I've never even looked very pregnant because I'm a slim build.

WHEN PREGNANCY MAKES YOU ILL

Whatever your male manager may be thinking about working mothers, or pregnant women, he'll certainly not be thrilled when you are absent due to sickness or physical problems with the pregnancy. This is where a woman has to be able to call on great inner strength to overcome her fears that she might lose either the job or her baby. And no one is making the situation easier for her.

For some women sufficiently senior in their place of work, the fear may express itself as one of losing hold or control. Gillian, one of the co-founders of a successful business, first pregnant at age 35 after two previous miscarriages, was rushed to hospital for two weeks and put on forced bed-rest with another threatened miscarriage. The timing was terrible, coinciding with a very important sales trip that had been planned long in advance:

> I had to cancel the whole trip the day before. More than sixty appointments. It was really difficult. Back at work, I think they as good as wrote me off. I felt so powerless and lay there worrying that this would be the end of my working life. That I'd have to stay in bed till the end of the pregnancy. Those first three months were truly awful.

For Sue, the London solicitor, who was unwillingly coping with the fears of single motherhood, the emotional maelstrom of that time was worsened by the physical problems she experienced during the pregnancy. Not only was she feeling vulnerable at work and in her failing relationship with the boy's father, but she had genuine anxieties, too, that she might lose the baby.

> At seven months, I was found to have *placenta previa* and had to stop working. I was in a pretty poor state by then, emotionally as well as physically, and I probably needed the time off. There were so many anxieties to cope with. Should I have the baby adopted? Would I miscarry? Was the baby going to be healthy? Would I be able to support the child alone?
>
> After I haemorrhaged I had to stop going to the office, though I could do some work from home. I was new in that job, scarcely eligible for maternity leave – but dependent on it. Then my employers said I had to take that sick leave as part of my maternity leave, which would have used most of it up before the baby even arrived! It was very difficult. Yet, after all that pain, the baby was born healthy and beautiful. He was almost magical – like a gift from God.

SORTING OUT THE FINANCIAL ARRANGEMENTS

Just how pregnancy and maternity leave is treated for working women is maybe one of the most disturbing factors. The women who participated in this book are for the most part happy with their working life, content with the arrangements and compromises, and they tend to look on the positive side of most of the consequent problems. However, there are times when even they crack the outer shell (of competence and control) and express openly their frustration, annoyance or anger at a system so patently unable to cope with women in senior positions preparing to take maternity leave.

Philippa is most outspoken – having gone through three difficult experiences of pregnancy – and now in a powerful position within a big company. The company's attitude, however, to her latest pregnancy reeked of old-world chauvinism.

At the time of my third pregnancy, I was a senior salesman on commission. They had never had a woman on commission taking maternity leave before. Also I was a woman manager of a department of nine other people, and they worried that my stand-in would not be able to handle the personnel side of my job. These may have been valid concerns. But they just did not know how to deal with the situation and I was horrified to find that in the late 1980s I was pioneering.

I was allowed to keep my company car. But, on commission, up to 20 per cent of your salary is made up of bonuses. They hadn't lowered my targets for the year and yet they wanted to pay me my salary, less a proportional amount of commission for the time I'd be on leave. In the end I threatened to make a big fuss. It was ridiculous. Effectively I'd have lost out because I was still aiming to achieve the year's targets.

Then, strictly speaking, if you are ill during pregnancy, that should count as part of your maternity leave. When I had to be in hospital for a few weeks towards the end of the pregnancy, my manager did try to help by monitoring me out sick for two of those weeks. But I'm a senior executive and shouldn't be treated this way!

If a man is out for five weeks with a heart attack, he just gets paid. They are very good on sick pay, in fact, for anyone – except pregnant women. The man would be on full pay for twenty-six weeks and then half pay thereafter. What made me really mad was that a male colleague was out having a hernia operation at the same time as I was going on maternity leave. He took six weeks off for his operation. And I was planning exactly the same time to have my baby. Not only was he on *full* pay, but he received full sympathy and support, whereas I was being put under pressure to take time off, to take a job with lower responsibility and not to be paid after six weeks.

That sort of thing really gets to me. When you're pregnant your hormones aren't 100 per cent on your side and your self-confidence is down. I wondered if I was being too emotional and so I tended not to take these things up with senior management because I was afraid of being seen as *emotional*. That was a difficult time. But my example has at least made things easier for other executive women taking maternity leave in our company now.

'They were treating me like a clerk/cashier'

Jane, the building society manager, has had a similar experience: both in feeling like a pioneer, and that she was being downgraded in the firm's attitude towards her maternity leave. Like Philippa and Sarah, she feels it has fallen on her shoulders to educate the company, to shake up the industry, so that women in the future won't meet so many obstacles:

Because I was the first woman manager ever to take maternity leave, I found they were treating me like a clerk/cashier. For example, they were going to put my staff interest rate mortgage on to the normal rate for those weeks I'd be away. It's pretty insulting. Really, they were assuming I wouldn't come back and covering themselves in case of that eventuality. The company car they also thought should go back for the sixteen weeks! My company just had not thought it through. They were making me into one of the girls. They've got to be brought into the 1990s.

WILL THEY PROMOTE YOU ONCE YOU'RE PREGNANT?

Advancement at work, once you begin having babies, is another thorny question; a briar patch that each woman has to negotiate herself. Not every woman even wants to think in terms of promotion when she is becoming a mother. She may be aware that she wants to have more than one child, and that now would be a good time to let her career simmer quietly for a few years. Yet other women find that it is only with motherhood that they begin to take their careers truly seriously:

> My career really only started the day I announced the pregnancy at the office. I'd been working full-time for several years by then, and I thought I was involved in a 'career'. But I realise now I had not begun to get serious. My real professional energy, drive and accomplishments are all inextricably linked to my having become a parent [says Lynne, a solicitor].
>
> But that took me by surprise, because I'd imagined either treading water while the child was young, or being so over-whelmed by it all that I might give up the job altogether. In effect, what happened to me was I gained new confidence, and maturity; I needed to earn a good living now, and that made me more ambitious. Also, I found I could be more productive at work; largely because my life was more well balanced. I really appreciated being in the office. And I looked forward to going home in the evening.

However, many women find things are not so easy. They are often angry at the subtle, or not so subtle, ways the newly pregnant woman is overlooked for promotions. The magazine editor, whom I mentioned at the beginning of the book, had already noticed that a promotion more or less promised her had now been quietly dropped:

> They had been planning to make me assistant editor. But I get the feeling now, I'm no longer in the running because I'm going to be taking maternity leave. I wouldn't dare fight it, though. You don't

have many grounds for such a fight when you're pregnant, do
you? The truth is they would be putting me into a much more
responsible position, at a time when the magazine is going all out
for promotion – and then I'd be leaving for up to six months.

Kathy, also a building society manager, noticed a very
definite change in attitudes towards her once she announced
she was pregnant:

> I notified my bosses as soon as possible that I was three months
> pregnant, to give them adequate time to find a temporary
> replacement for my job. Then a promotional opportunity pre-
> sented itself and I expressed an interest in applying for the
> vacancy. I was told an application would not be accepted from
> me. The reason given was that the office had been without an
> assistant manager for some time, and that to appoint someone
> who was shortly going to be on maternity leave would not be
> practical.
>
> I thought of appealing, depending on the shortlist for the job.
> They had allowed at least two other people much less experienced
> than myself to apply. But in the end they appointed someone who
> had had a similar level of experience, so I did not argue my case.
> Apart from that, I noticed that my senior line manager was quite
> paternalistic about my plan to return to work. He really didn't
> appreciate that I was serious.

'It's as though you're declaring a moratorium on your career'

Megan, at 44, has just parleyed her management position into
a job-share with a colleague in the same department. She is
frank about the stress of returning to full-time work once her
baby is 6 months old. The situation feels much better with the
reduced working week and the job-share – despite her loss of
pay and status.

For Megan, herself, the job-share in fact involved a demo-
tion. The colleague was not at her same level and, when they
analysed the situation carefully, they felt it would be better to
share the lesser position – to avoid her partner being promoted to Megan's level:

The minute you begin on something like a job-share, you have to be prepared to miss out on promotions. It's as though you're declaring a moratorium on your career. People are inclined to write you off, bypass you. They don't take you as seriously, on the assumption you've lost interest. So you do have to work at that.

There are not many women at my level in the company. I began here eighteen years ago, just out of school, as a wages clerk. I've worked my way up. But I'm quite content about the situation, as I knew I just couldn't manage the stress of full-time work and motherhood. So it's a fact of life I'm prepared to live with.

What I did find difficult was another inevitable fact of life – the man they put in as my stand-in when I was on maternity leave is now my *boss*. Of course I don't feel he does the job half as well as I used to. But that's my problem. I chose to make this change.

AMBITION FOR WORKING MOTHERS DOES NOT RING OF TRADITIONAL 'FEMININITY'

Promotion, fighting to get to the top, being determined to continue pushing up the career ladder through pregnancies or while your children are young, are topics that most women are still afraid to address. They do not ring with traditional concepts of femininity, and more often than not the career-mother will hide her true feelings, especially from other female colleagues.

Naomi, in her mid 30s with a 2-year-old son, works for a museum of cultural affairs. Right now she is contemplating having a second child. But she is also considering career advancement:

I am ambitious. I know it's unusual for women to admit to it, as though it were a dirty word. But frankly I could do my boss's job and my director's. Yet I could also soft-pedal or move into a new field while I'm having children. I enjoy work, recognition and being paid – I'm also very proud of the sort of position I've achieved.

I'm trying to work out when to get pregnant again as there is a possibility, when a senior retires, of promotion. I don't believe they'd give it to me if I were pregnant. I've heard their comments on this in regards to other women here. I want everything at once: to have another baby, change jobs, be promoted. I know I can't plan for it, so I'll just go out and see what I can get.

'Never act apologetically ... stand your ground'

Depending on your line of work, seniority and level of respect in which you are held, or if you work for yourself either in business or in a creative capacity, having children just may, as Lynne mentioned previously, increase your self-confidence and marketability.

Celia, the designer who manages to combine a very well-paid career, based at home, with motherhood of two daughters aged 11 and under 1 year, is a prime example:

> Both times I've been pregnant have also been career peaks for me; I've been offered new positions with greater responsibility and higher pay. Don't ask me why – looking back I think I was just lucky in my timing. If I'd accepted the greater responsibility first, I might never have dared get pregnant, either time!
>
> The first time, I was working in an office, and I was able to use the better job offer to blackmail my boss into letting me work a three-day week once the baby was born. Once I'd achieved that promise, I noticed a lot of grumbling about how 'Celia is never in the office any more'. It taught me a big lesson: even if you achieve a deal like that you have to outface them, and never act apologetically about it. When you're beginning to feel paranoid about their attitude you must stand your ground and remind them of the deal and *why* it was worked out.
>
> As a working mother, you'll be dealing with a lot of imponderables. The male boss may have a wife at home and have very mixed feelings about women working anyway, and particularly mothers. You may have a boss who is a working woman with no children, who resents you being favoured in any way. Or, what can be worse, the female boss who had children years ago – but left hers at home with a nanny, to concentrate on career – now feels threatened by you. So you're flat up against her *guilt*.
>
> Most colleagues, particularly men, are oblivious to what it is really like to be pregnant or have a child. Because I work from home and they don't see me all the time, I think they imagine I'm

lazing around with my feet up. They phone up with their demands. And there are times when I feel very pressured to keep up the volume of work.

During this recent pregnancy, for example, I covered myself for six weeks' worth of work in advance – which I put together during the tiredness of the pregnancy – so that I could guarantee a quiet time with the baby. One day when I was phoned and asked to produce something extra that day, I had to remind the man politely that I was booked in for a C-section that afternoon. He said, 'But it's really urgent. C-sections are easier than they used to be, aren't they?' I pointed out it still means being cut open. And he left the conversation, lamely adding, 'Rather you than me!'

I must say I don't feel so ambitious any more. I hit a change around 40 – after years of being a real workaholic. I used to work to the detriment of my marriage and of my elder daughter. Far from seeing work from home as an easy opt out, while she was at school I'd work all day. Then I'd take off the late afternoon and early evening, and return to my work from 9 p.m.–1 a.m. This time around, with the new baby, I'm just not doing all that. If I look back, I can see it was madness. A sort of half life.

6   GOING BACK TO WORK

The baby has been the dominant force in your life since the moment you either conceived, or planned to try to become pregnant. This new stage of life you have entered or are now entering will engage a major shift in your priorities, loyalties and commitments. Whether you were determined to return to work immediately, or whether you have managed to fit in an extended maternity leave as the best of all options, this is the moment that, following the birth itself, you have been nervously waiting for.

How much time you will have taken off from work on maternity leave may have been prejudged by the type of work, your employer, or other mitigating factors such as your need for money. It may equally have been predetermined by your views of yourself as a mother – how long you feel you need to stay at home full time with the new baby.

Just what are the right, or acceptable, amounts of time, are imponderable questions, for which there are no easy answers. What is right for one woman and her situation will be wrong for another. From the women I interviewed, there came a wide variety of responses to the questions: 'How long a maternity leave did you take?' and 'Do you regret that particular choice of length of time?'

In certain careers – such as regular retail banking, teaching and the civil service – where career breaks are allowed and understood, the women who choose to take a year or more out of the workplace are not penalised. They are welcomed back to a similar job, at similar seniority and pay level. In other instances, mentioned earlier in the book, women are penalised by taking time off. They lose out on the career ladder race and have to mark time for those years, being passed over for promotions and pay rises.

Jane, the building society manager, felt that career breaks, available for up to two to five years in her industry, are in principle a good idea:

But, in reality if you take such a long time off, you really do lose out. After six months, for example, you'd lose not only steps on the career ladder but also your self-confidence. It all comes down to having to decide just what you want. Just imagine taking five years out in today's market. You'd have to be extraordinarily self-confident to republicise yourself again, to push your profile to the point of real credibility.

As I was the first female manager ever to take maternity leave, I was able to negotiate my time out. They wouldn't really have had to give me my old position back. They could get away with offering me another branch at the same grade. So I'm returning quickly, to slide straight back in. I'd be afraid to take a longer time off and then go back full time. I wouldn't be able to perform properly.

'I never got myself out of the working frame of mind'

Certain women are able to combine career and motherhood by continuing to work from home in the early weeks. Ellen, in the previous chapter, was an extreme case. Highly valued in her small company, she agreed to take no maternity leave and to keep up her work from home. Anne, in management as a salesman with a computer company, remarked that her male colleagues proved quite co-operative in the long run:

They came for meetings at my house. I had been given a special job on a new product and even though, for the first meeting at home, I wasn't really there, mentally, it was reassuring to know I could keep up with the work. My husband stayed at home and cooked lunch. My manager was late. But it was quite a jolly time.

During my second pregnancy, I took just two weeks off before the birth and two weeks afterwards. There were only two to three days when my manager had to visit me at home. I feel you lose out if you take off longer. I could, in fact, have taken a full nine months and held on to my position. But my attitude is all about me and this damned ladder I feel I am on. People said to me you'll feel terrible that day you return to work. But I didn't. I never got myself out of the working frame of mind.

'If you stay away too long ... you'd give up control'

Gillian, co-founder of a company and in a very senior position, took off three weeks to a month altogether, but found she was back on the phone to the office after a week:

> You can't stay away too long. If you do, you'd give up control. I had to remain in touch, be there to solve problems. It's all very political. Besides I found dealing with my daughter a chore at the time. She cried a lot. In fact, after being ill and tired so much during the pregnancy, I had a new boost of energy when I got back to work. Once I was over breastfeeding, I really bounced back. I honestly used to forget about my baby during the working day. Then at 4 p.m., I'd suddenly remember, 'Oh, I have a daughter.' That was when she was an infant, and basically needed a nurturer. Now she is nearly 3, it's a lot more of a problem. I can't shut her out of my life in the same way.

MANY WOMEN FEEL THE NEED TO RETURN TO WORK EARLY

For Christine, the doctor in charge of an area health district, who had her baby at age 37 and resumed full-time work at four weeks, 'My attitude to work or my colleagues really never changed.' And for Kathy, the other building society manager, who took off two months before the birth and three and a half months afterwards: 'It was too long for me. I was desperate to get back to work, and found being at home very boring. I had a tendency to be introspective.'

Judy, who is with a major international bank and has a 1-year-old baby, and puts in as long a day as any man, took off a full six months, including a couple of weeks beforehand. But she panicked:

After three months or so, I was desperate to get out of the house, to get out of the situation. I felt completely ground down being home with a crying baby, not being recognised or being paid.

In physical terms, looking back, I'm glad I took that long a break because if I'd tried to go back earlier I wouldn't have been able to keep up to standard. It was my mentor/partner in the organisation who encouraged me to take such a long time as he said I should be relaxed about my return. I was pleased because after six months back at work he felt I'd re-established myself.

JUST LONG ENOUGH. TOO LONG AND YOU'RE BORED AND RESTLESS

Philippa, in her high-powered management role with a major multinational, believes in taking just long enough:

Too long, and you become bored and restless. Too short, and you're overtired when you return. With my third baby, I was out for seven weeks; that was just about right. Five weeks, with the second, was slightly too early. With the first baby, when I took a full maternity leave and removed myself from the career ladder, I had to face up to the fact that just wasn't for me.

FOR OTHERS, A SLOW RETURN IS A MORE BALANCED OPTION

Sometimes the women who have been able to move slowly back into the workplace seem the most balanced. Naomi, for example, who is equally forthright about being ambitious, feels that her leave of four months before returning to part-time status, and full-time at six months, was perhaps slightly too short: 'I should have waited longer, but money was tight.'

Whereas Dee, senior editor at a publisher, feels content with her compromise:

I worked right up to the time of birth. If I'd gone into labour eight hours later, I would really have been at my desk! Then I continued with bits and pieces from home a couple of weeks after he was born. I went into the office, with the baby, at least once a week from five weeks. Then I returned for two full days a week from five months; and really full time from seven months.

Larraine, the European politican with three young children, took ten weeks off with her first baby – which really could have been six months if she hadn't been so fraught about leaving work for too long. By the time she was having her third, she did take a full six months' leave – but she was able to fit that in comfortably.

BACK TO WORK AND TO A REAL WELCOME – OR NOT?

And there we are, on the first day back, trying hard to look slim and self-confident in a suit that is either a pared-down maternity suit made to look thinner, or one from a previous life, trying desperately to conceal the bulges. There we are nervously holding the briefcase, folder, notes, hoping all will be well and that we won't feel choked with tears, or worry about the childcare, or leak with milk. There we are wondering if former colleagues will treat us sympathetically; or glare at us with ill-concealed resentment and hostility.

Some women find the return to work not only difficult because of the inevitable guilt and conflict of loyalties, but also because colleagues or bosses do not make that return any easier. And these women may not be the clerks or assistants – but just as likely those who hold high-paying, senior positions.

'My stand-in said: "What are you doing here?"'

Philippa, who was under extreme pressure, holding down a crucial position as a salesman, a very visible spot that had to be rescued. Altogether she took seven weeks' maternity leave.

As this was her third baby, Philippa knew what she was confronting and had hired a live-in nanny. She was looking forward to returning to her career, very happy and well supported by her new husband, and feeling she had spent long enough at home full time with the baby:

> We had agreed on when I'd go back. It had all been discussed. But the day I went in my stand-in said, 'What are you doing here?' He thought he had the job for the rest of the year.
>
> I was very uptight, needless to say. Instead, they offered me work on a special taskforce that was being set up. In itself it wasn't a bad career move, but it was away from the department I'd been so involved with. I was torn between what to do, but in the end decided to keep my nose clean and toe the company line. I found it very, very difficult, though. I knew I was swallowing far too much.
>
> Driving up the motorway to that job, I used to imagine all sorts of conversations with my managers. It was very stressful. They had also promised me a promotion at the end of the year, but that was overlooked. In my experience, when you return to work you have to prove yourself all over again. In retrospect, I probably lost at least six months in career progression, though I have managed to catch up since. But that might be luck or simply that my attitude remained healthy. Really, all I did was take a few weeks off, and I never asked for any concessions as a working mother.

'It was as if I had no track record'

Sarah, the accountant with a major national industry, and mother of 5- and 2-year-olds, found that her experience on returning to her prestigious position, after the second maternity leave, changed her attitude to work, and the company, for ever:

> I was so angry. I was absolutely livid. I'd planned, thought about and talked to people about my maternity leave. I was organised to work part time from home at first. I'd offered myself for four hours a day. But no one made use of me. Then, I had appendicitis within the last month of maternity leave and that rather ruined those plans. But I could not believe the lack of imagination and

sympathy on the part of my company. I was due to come back on a Friday – but as I had been ill I asked if I could make it the Monday instead. The Personnel Officer said no, I had to appear on the Friday as the appendicitis was part of maternity leave!

Then, because I had moved to a new department, I discovered they hadn't organised my job at all. It was as if I had no track record. It made me change my attitude to the company very dramatically.

I knew I couldn't let them walk over me. I was angry but that was not constructive. There wasn't anything I could do with the anger, other than find a new job in another department and start all over again. So, now that I've been given the opportunity to make a sideways move and work part time as a consultant, I've happily accepted the new situation. And I'll see what happens to the rest of my career or working life.

CHANGING YOUR ATTITUDE TO THE JOB; AND STICKING WITH IT

Other women have also found that the attitude of maybe just one male manager, or the company undergoing reorganisation, can make the atmosphere very different when they return to work after maternity leave. The difference in your personal status now as a mother – in their terms meaning you will no longer be 100 per cent loyal to the company – will also be out to defeat you. The newly returned working mother may feel the tension and fail to perform as she is remembered or expected.

'On the verge of tears, I had to keep up my professional image'

Laura, aged 33, was a well-regarded computer technologist with a leading chemical company. During her first pregnancy and maternity leave she had no problems. But the new director who once had favoured her changed his attitude from the moment she announced the second pregnancy:

He acted as if I had failed him. To constantly test me, he would assign triple the work to me, as compared to my colleagues. I never failed to complete the work but he just kept pouring it on, even to my last day before maternity leave. I was always on the verge of tears, but I had to keep up the professional image.

Men are either in awe of working mothers or they think we are crazy. Although I'd looked forward to returning to work after my first pregnancy, I dreaded coming back the second time. My director treated me as a second-rate professional, someone not to be depended on, since I had taken a three-month maternity leave.

But the whole atmosphere of the company had changed. Promotions were now being given mostly by who you knew, not how skilled you were. So I learned no longer to think of myself as having a career. It's just a job now. I do what is required of me and nothing more. My former director was forced out, and now my manager is no better. Since I don't have a scientific degree, I no longer fit into the scheme of things.

The situation is beyond my control and in order to survive this time emotionally, I have placed my family as number one in my life, and career as number two. I'm sure my manager would be thrilled if I left but I'm a fighter and I won't give him the satisfaction.

SOLUTIONS TO AN OVERLY STRESSFUL SITUATION

Even a high-flyer career woman may find that returning to work full time, once she's had a baby, is just too much in terms of the hours that are available in the day, emotional and psychological stressors. Deep down this woman may want to be at home with her baby. Because no woman can ever prejudge this feeling (or, those who do simply take themselves out of the workplace to begin with), the best advice is that any woman should ideally be able to keep her options open – although, as we have seen in the previous stories, it is very often this Catch-22 situation that leads to male managers' and colleagues' negative reaction to the idea of working mothers.

The woman in the following story found the ultimate in satisfactory solutions. The situation suited her and her bosses.

The compromises were shared. Hers is a happy tale, but still sadly all too rare.

'A successful job-share'

Forty-four-year-old Megan, mother of a 2-year-old, found herself under those particular pressures when she returned to full-time work, six months after her daughter's birth. Megan was in a senior position, one of only four women with a large national company. Her good fortune was to be in a position – in regulatory law – for which there are few people equally trained, let alone female or male. Her talents were very much needed. Her bargaining power was strong.

At one point, Megan seriously considered resigning because she felt so stressed being away for such long hours from her daughter, and leaving her with a nanny she did not trust. However, instead, Megan was able to put up a case for a job-share with one of her colleagues. Their plans were immediately and quite happily accepted by senior management. More on the creation of this job-share will be discussed in Chapter 10. But this is how Megan describes the situation that led to her near resignation:

> I'd worked a long time in quite a senior position and I thought I'd be able to handle full-time working motherhood quite easily. This is my second marriage, and as I was 40 at the time of the pregnancy, I'm quite old to be a first-time mother. Until that point my career had been my life, and I didn't imagine any change.
>
> I had been used to working long days from 7.30 a.m. to 7.30 p.m., but I soon found that even cutting back on my hours didn't mean I saw my daughter any more – except to tuck her into bed at night. I also felt I wasn't handling my job as well as I used to. So I was finding it very stressful; not doing anything to the best of my ability.
>
> That nine months of Susanna's life that I worked full time I now see as one of the worst nightmares of my life. I took it out mostly on my husband, resenting the way he only had to cope with his job, nothing changed for him at home. Then the situation was resolved by a woman in my department telling me she was

planning to become pregnant. She could see how stressed I was, that it just wasn't working out for me, and asked if I would consider doing a job-share? We'd worked together for five years and are friends. So we believed it could work very well.

Immediately I took to the idea, but we were both nervous of its reception.

RETURNING TO WORK AFTER A LONG BREAK

When women in the past took five or maybe ten years out of the workforce to bring up their children at home, few gave serious consideration as to how they were ever to re-enter this same workforce. The results of that negligence or ignorance (the majority assumed they might never need to return to work – unless divorce or widowhood came in to spoil the picture) have been all too obvious to ensuing generations. Women have watched their mothers, grandmothers and female colleagues shunted to the sidelines, given low-paying, low-interest and low-responsibility jobs.

But, if today's woman decided to take a 'long' break – by which I would mean a year or more after the birth of her children – is the moving back in any easier?

'I was disparaged as a freelance who would not be able to work with others'

Maryanne, whom we met earlier in the book, is quite typical of a certain type of talented and well-educated woman. Now turned 40, with children aged 9 and 7, she began her working life on newspapers, but took several years out of the full-time workforce to work as a freelance, based at home, when her children were growing up.

Nearing 40, she began to feel the cold wind at their doorstep, especially as they had just moved out of the city to a big house in a country town. The instability of freelance life, and insecurity over when cheques would arrive, led Maryanne to make an all out effort to get back into the full-time workforce:

It was very hard. People in power would look at my CV, which had an incredible amount on it for the years in which my children were small – five books, hundreds of major magazine articles, PR and promotion for several big companies and, in fact, a two-year stretch when I worked full time, albeit on a daily basis, for two corporate PR firms. And, on the side, if you can believe it, I wrote 300 articles for a major newspaper too!

I made a lot of money in some of those years, but when I tried to parley that experience into a full-time job, I was disparaged as a freelance who would not be able to work with others.

Prospective employers would marvel at my tenacity and productivity, but muttered about how the independent spirit that engendered all that work wouldn't fit in the 'real' world of work. I really believe that discrimination is practised against women with children who make career turns that don't follow prescribed routes. I used to explain patiently to interviewers that a freelance contractor must, in fact, be able to work with many different personalities, often at once. It didn't seem to please them and they were probably intimidated that I was juggling so much, so well!

Now I am finally back as TV and entertainments editor of a big newspaper. I sometimes wonder why I was hired, but I think it was due not only to the desperation of a particular boss (he needed to fill the position within a week and I was 'available') but also because he was recently divorced, had a preschool child, and could sympathise with my desire and need for full-time work. I was pretty straight about wanting the job and needing to prove erroneous the suspicions that my skills wouldn't be adaptable to an office. I've worked bloody hard since I came here, I can tell you!

FOREVER HAVING TO 'PROVE' YOURSELF OVER AGAIN

The 'patchwork' career referred to in Chapter 4, so common for women, can also lead to some very frustrating moments of trying to prove oneself all over again. This can be particularly true if you move countries or cities with a husband, trying desperately to look for work with each move.

Angela, who is 34, and mother to three young children

under 7, began her adult life with a BA degree, with distinction, in English language and literature. First, after teacher training, she taught English in a secondary school. But then the family moved to another town, she gave birth to her eldest son, and began instead to work for a small advertising agency. Finally, after the third child, she worked as a sales representative for a greetings card company. Now, she has given up work entirely – for as long as they can afford for her to be out of work:

> Motherhood has meant so many interruptions for me, with no promise of a job after maternity leave. I feel I've had a series of jobs rather than a single-focus career. Also, being a woman prevented my being promoted with the advertising agency that deals with many industrial accounts.
>
> Twice I had to leave jobs to take maternity leave of more than six months – the jobs themselves just wouldn't be available after that time. And all my leave was unpaid. Changing careers was very upsetting and going back into teaching was tough. Sales was also a whole new field for me; frightening and pressured. I find that getting interviews for new jobs is the problem. It takes a lot of time to unearth a decent well-paying job – particularly at my age and with my experience.

In the next two chapters, I will be looking at the stories of women who have experienced extreme responses to work and motherhood. First, there are the two women who found themselves being forced out of work because of pregnancy or motherhood. Second, two women who have decided to devote the foreseeable future to bringing up their children while working at home.

7 ... OR BACKS TO THE WALL?

Most Western countries now have legislation protecting the rights of women to continue working throughout their pregnancies and allowing their return after an agreed amount of maternity leave to a position at least as good as the one they left behind. The very different levels of legislative protection in certain countries has long made women angry. (For more information on this topic see *New Mothers at Work* by Peter Moss (Unwin Hyman, 1988) and Sylvia Ann Hewlett's *A Lesser Life* (Michael Joseph, 1987).)

Female cynics in most countries are aware that ways and means can be adopted to force a woman out of her position — if not out of work altogether — should her bosses or colleagues decide to apply unfair emotional or psychological pressures to the new mother.

Having to bear with such difficulties at a time when any woman would be in no fit state to fight is, in itself, unfair. To cope with emotionally fraught situations, when her hormones are leaving her weak and vulnerable, and when her self-confidence might be low because of a changing sense of identity, is expecting too much of the pregnant woman.

One of the major inequities of this situation is, as many women have pointed out, that male colleagues may well take a longer time than statutory maternity leave off from work, on account of serious illnesses such as heart disease or stress, or because they need a sabbatical to work through some personal problem. Men seem to receive such leave without penalty, whilst women are frowned upon for their pregnancies, for no longer being 'just like men'.

Esther is now 42, a large, attractive and well-dressed woman, seemingly self-confident and self-possessed, who is mother to a 6-year-old daughter and a 9-month-old son. Esther's most recent position was as general manager of a laboratory connected with the textile industry – a company that had been very badly run until its recent take-over by a multinational parent group.

Telling her story still brings out in Esther an ill-concealed rage. With her career something of a shambles, she is trying to pick up the pieces of the past few years' work and experience, to set up on her own as a consultant. Esther was definitely forced out of her job because of her pregnancy – and in no gentle or even very subtle fashion.

'They were hoping I'd just walk out under the pressure'

When you're seen as tough and successful at work, they imagine that's what you're like as a woman. It doesn't help me that I'm 5 ft 10 in tall, quite outspoken, and not at all I suppose in the traditional mould of 'feminine' woman. I'm proud of the fact I rallied under the stress, but to have to go through all that when I was pregnant was almost more than I could possibly stand.

My career has followed a strange track. I was not fully educated because my parents seemed to think girls only needed to find a man and get married. How wrong they were! I left school and took a secretarial course, later polishing this up with a commercial course in foreign languages. Somehow I slid into the textile industry, as an administrative assistant. By this time, in my late 20s, I had begun to focus on a career as children had not come along (though I was married at 22 to my first husband).

Soon, I was running the marketing department of a small textile company, and then I was head-hunted to a larger firm. By then, I was design-sourcing and selling to major stores. I found it creative and really enjoyable work and was becoming quite well known within the industry.

I became pregnant for the first time at 34, and I gave up that job as it entailed a lot of transatlantic travelling – to America once every two weeks. I just knew I could not do that with a baby. It was very much an all or nothing type of job. So I freelanced for a while, then with my new husband moved to America to try to set up in business there. The amount of work available was promising but we simply could not get legal papers to stay – so we returned.

I picked up the pieces of my work again, and moved outside the city, to join a small company that had been set up by four men – all of whom had been made redundant from other firms. None of them had any marketing skills and the whole place was riddled by confusion as none would take superiority over the others.

I couldn't take all this in-fighting and, besides, I wasn't very impressed with their ideas or working standards. So again I left to become freelance. That company was eventually bought up by the multinational conglomerate and I was invited back to *run* it. It seemed the right thing to do, as again it meant we could live outside the city (by now I was a single parent and needed a steady income, too). It was tricky as I was going back over the heads of these same four men, for whom I had originally worked, as their general manager.

As far as I could see, I did a good job there, but the company itself had terrible problems which the conglomerate had never really focused on. By this time remarried, and personally very happy, I became pregnant again at the age of 41. I hadn't been with the company long enough for maternity leave, and I really had no intention of giving up my career, so I simply planned on working through to the end of the pregnancy, and then to take *no* maternity leave – just four weeks made up of holiday and unpaid leave.

My immediate bosses were out in the Middle East, though the conglomerate's head office was in London. I sent memos to my Middle Eastern bosses telling them of my plans. And I had no response. By the fifth month, I'd begun to think I should get something in writing. I sent a fax to the Middle East asking for confirmation of my plans. The very next morning a note landed on my desk from the conglomerate's chief executive, informing me that when I took off to have my baby in September I would not be invited back!

I rang them up and demanded to know what was going on. I explained that I was not taking leave for the baby – only a couple of weeks' vacation and a couple more weeks' unpaid leave. The unhealthy men I had been working with, I pointed out, had had more than that amount of time off in recent months – for back problems and asthma. Fortunately, I was strong enough to fight for my rights and demand a hearing.

The next few weeks were horrendous – emotionally draining and, I felt, very demeaning. There was a series of meetings to which I took a tape recorder hidden in my bra. I was always outnumbered by two or three men. Basically, they were hoping I'd just walk out under the pressure. But I knew if I did there would be no financial compensation. I just was not going to have them use my *pregnancy* as a reason to fire me.

Although I'm not the type to dissolve in tears, there were times in those meetings when I could have crumpled. No one was there to help me. I was working only with other men, no other women were at my level. Even my husband didn't seem to feel he should jump in to my rescue. I was left to fight this out all on my own. And I was worried, despite being healthy, that at aged 41, and as I had threatened miscarriage twice before – there is always a risk of high blood pressure – that the stress and strain might make me lose the baby.

But I also felt that they had robbed me of my brain. Being large and bulbous became a diminishing experience for me – they could now only see me as a *reproductive* woman, not as a thinking person, full of creativity and ideas. I didn't want to lose my job, but I didn't want to have this fight either.

Legally they were within their rights to lay me off if my work was not good enough. But they would then have to pay me redundancy. They were making use of the notion that I was taking maternity leave not to invite me back.

By the time we got into discussions, it was obvious someone had made a very inept decision and they all pretended not to know where the original directive had come from. Eventually it was sorted out at a high level. I was given six months' severance pay. They tried, at the seventh month of pregnancy, to offer me a different position within the company, to which they felt I could return after motherhood. But by then I had no desire to continue working with them.

Maybe a pregnant managing director was going to be an embarrassment – I wish they had come right out and said so. Since having the baby, I have again freelanced and am now setting myself up in business on a consultancy basis. I tried going for interviews, for a full-time position again, just to restore my self-confidence. But I find now with two children, and a husband who works long hours, that I cannot imagine hiring someone efficient enough to take care of my children who will also be able to run the house and family for twelve hours a day from 7 a.m.–7 p.m. I'll basically continue to work from a home-based business. I can't see any other way.

I think a lot of women like me are struggling hard to keep up our end in the working world. And a lot of men are fighting just as hard to make things impossible for us. If a man was put on the spot, because he'd had a heart attack, told not to come back, that they didn't feel he was capable of doing the job any more, there would be all sorts of trouble, wouldn't there?

'I stayed five months until I could not take the pressures any more'

For other women, it's the experience of returning to work that leads to the uncomfortable sensation that they are being eased out. There are the old jokes of the executive who goes on holiday, only to find no desk on her or his return. Similarly, the woman who takes off for a long maternity leave may find herself returning to an untenable position. Should she stay and fight for her rights? Is she left wanting to remain with that company?

Very often these situations occur where a company has been taken over by a conglomerate; where all positions and roles are in a state of flux; where former bosses are long gone and the atmosphere once known and maybe loved has changed absolutely. Just how much strength a pregnant woman, or new mother, can muster to handle the very obvious bad vibes is in question here.

Anya, aged 38, for seven years held down a very responsible job as head of advertising and public relations with a multi-national bank, which was undergoing rapid expansion at the time she became pregnant. She feels now that she was forced out of her position on returning after a twelve-month maternity leave:

The bank was undergoing an enormous transition at the time I fell pregnant. My area of advertising and public relations was to double in budget. I should point out that, for most of my years with the bank, I was the *only* senior female executive. It was a very chauvinistic company, very much in the public school image, and they simply tolerated me because I was in an area they knew nothing about. Special committees were being formed to map out the new bank. Anyone gaining a position on the committee was expected to be given even higher status, once they started their new operations.

However, although they had hinted I would be given a place on one of these new committees, once I announced my pregnancy and plan to take a twelve-month maternity leave, I was told this was no longer possible. It was a very bad time to be leaving the company, and I really think female executives should not expect to walk out on a senior role, and to walk back into it after twelve months away, without sufficient planning.

I mapped out a plan for my absence, which divided the job into two roles. I appointed a new advertising manager from outside the company. The public relations role would be carried out by an external consultancy firm. When I returned I would take on the internal public relations role. The two roles would work in liaison, reporting to a deputy managing director. I left two months before the birth of our son, having been asked to stay as long as possible to brief the new appointments.

During my absence, I kept in touch with the new advertising manager, who was having one problem after another. As a woman, she found the company the most male chauvinist she had ever known, and she was no spring chicken either. After six months, she resigned. They asked me to come back then, but I refused.

Once my twelve months were up, I contacted the bank to discuss my return, to find I was talking to new people. All the executives were new. I asked for a pay increase, on the basis that my salary would have risen over the last twelve months, plus a company car and expense account for entertaining. This was all agreed to. I asked for our discussions to be covered in writing, and I would send in a written confirmation of acceptance.

The letter arrived, but the terms were not as discussed. I was to return on the same salary, no company car (the rules had changed in the year) and no expense account at present. I was very annoyed and immediately made different contacts higher up. They agreed, finally, on the salary increase but the car and expenses were out. I tried to find an alternative position – and although I was always shortlisted down to the last three, I was not successful. So I returned to the bank.

I considered contacting the Equal Opportunities Commission; over the phone they thought I had a case. I seriously thought about fighting for my rights, but even if I had won, it would have been a pyrrhic victory. There would have been publicity about the case, and that would have done *me* more personal harm than the company. Who would want to employ a trouble-maker? Also the stress involved was not going to be worth the effort.

8 HOME-BASED MOTHERS: WHEN MOTHERING IS FIRST PRIORITY

The women who speak openly in favour of home-based mothering – full time, no excuses, no guilt or conflicts over who they are, whether they are 'wasting' their adult years, whether they are right and working mothers are wrong – are a rarity these days. The majority of women who do spend a few years home based, while children are young, tend to turn to some form of self-employment, voluntary work or entre-preneurial activity. They are in effect only biding their time until they can transfer those skills back into the workforce. But, the rarities do still exist and no doubt will continue to do so. There is, after all, room for choice in today's world.

Here, I am pinpointing two different kinds of stories. Melanie is a mother agonising about whether she should return to work and, if she makes that decision, how will it be possible. Anya, whom we met in the previous chapter, we left at the point of deciding to give up the struggle with an overly stressful full-time career. Perhaps surprisingly, she made the move back to full-time mothering.

'There's no doubt about it – I'm scared'

Melanie, who is now 28, describes her situation, her conflicts, this way:

> As I am not currently working, I cannot really talk about being a mother and having a career. However, I am now – and have been for some time – going through a phase that might often precede a

mother's return to work: that is the dilemma a woman experiences while deciding whether to continue being a full-time mother or to go back to full-time or part-time work.

My son has just turned 5 and I have had no job except caring for him, my husband and the household since he was born. Long ago I accepted the fact that having a child meant that my life would no longer be entirely my own. For a while I was quite content with my role as mother and housewife. My son was, and still is, quite a demanding child and taking care of him seemed to fill the entire day. I went to bed each night satisfied that I had done my job as mother and housewife well that day.

But things began changing when he started school over a year ago. He only goes to preschool from 9 a.m. to 12 noon but the extra time on my hands has forced me to question whether I am really doing enough. I no longer feel fully satisfied that I am achieving everything I was supposed to, or could be accomplishing. Everywhere I look – on TV, in newspapers and magazines, etc. – I see that 'today's woman' is not just a stay-at-home mother; she is a talented, financially successful, effervescent career woman, *and* mother of one or more children. And here am I, a woman at home with just one child, living comfortably and being fully provided for by my husband.

I tried to justify my right to feel comfortable with my life as it was. I figured that since my husband was almost always away (he has averaged over 200 days per year out-of-town for his job since our son was born), I was not just a mother but practically a father too. Unfortunately my line of thinking backfired, and I began to realise how unfair it was that my husband was working so hard to make a living, that he had hardly any life besides his job at all. I felt that I should be working, too.

To tell the truth, it wasn't just a desire to earn money that was bothering me, but I felt a need to get out into the world again, and be in contact with people of my age group who might offer more stimulating conversation than an update on their children's daily behaviour. Loving and caring for a young child all day long, every day, practically all by myself and with very little other social stimulation, was simply not fulfilling me emotionally or mentally.

As a result, I enrolled in a computer-training course at a local adult education centre a few months after my son started school. It was my first attempt at least to make myself feel as if I was doing something towards a more productive goal. I completed the course, but did not even try to look for a job after that. Why? Because of the following questions impossible to answer: How could I go back to work? Who would take care of my son before and after school? How would I manage the household chores of cooking and cleaning? Would it be fair to my son to leave him in the care of a sitter when, financially, I really didn't have to work? Part-time work was not the answer, either, as the types of jobs available would hardly pay for a working woman's wardrobe, let alone a babysitter or childminder, for even part of the day.

Six months went by before I took any further steps towards getting a job. Then I started another course, to become an estate agent. Towards the end, I was asked by the instructor if I would like to participate in a sales training course at the large estate agency where he worked. Since then I have been attending these meetings weekly.

I could take on a job there any time. But I still cannot commit myself because I have not yet worked out who would take care of my son – especially in this field which would take me away from my family for many evenings and at weekends. Nor have I figured out how not to feel guilty about leaving him in the care of someone else.

Even if I did get past those two obstacles, I worry whether I would still have the energy and time after work to read to, play with, talk to and listen to my son with sufficient quality and quantity to consider myself a good mother. Still beyond that, would I have enough time and energy left after all this to give my husband the love and attention that he deserves and that I would want to give him?

I know it's not going to be easy having a job *and* doing all the things I've been doing for the past five years at home. And there's no doubt about it – I'm scared. I'm afraid of failing on the job, or worse yet, as a wife and mother. As it now looks, I'll continue with the estate agency training, but I think I'll wait until my son starts full-time school, in the autumn, before I begin working even part time.

Until then, I'll keep trying to be the best mother I know how to be. After all, what job could possibly have rewards any greater than watching your child develop into a warm and wonderful human being, while knowing that you played a very significant part in that development?

'I always thought I'd be more happy with a career than with children'

Thirty-eight-year-old Anya, in the previous chapter, discussed with unconcealed bitterness her reactions to the male-dominated international banking company she had worked with for seven years before the birth of her son (who is now 2½ years old).

The surprise to Anya was less that she enjoyed motherhood but, when faced with a hostile work environment and the unending problems of childcare and hours, she has found herself far happier staying home and dedicating her life to her son:

> My husband and I left starting a family until later in life because we simply were not interested in children. We had been married ten years, had a good relationship, and enjoyed the living standard one does with two good incomes: the best restaurants and several holidays a year. We felt children would be a hindrance to our lifestyle. To be frank, I always thought I'd be more happy with a career than with children. However, during our 30s, we began to wonder whether we might regret not having children when we were older. So we took the plunge, both feeling we were ready for a change of pace.
>
> Having had my son has made me a much more thoughtful person, particularly towards other mothers. It has also made me realise there is more to life than just working and earning money. They have now become very low on my list of priorities.
>
> In the long run, when I did return to work, I found an almost different company, with staff morale very low. I cannot say whether or not my ability was viewed differently, because most of the senior managers whom I had worked with had left. So I was in a position where I had to prove myself all over again.
>
> Maybe I also no longer had the same incentive. Maybe it was the company's attitude towards me, the staff's low morale, or the fact that deep down I would rather have been at home with my little boy. Perhaps it was a combination of all three.
>
> My job was never a neat 9 a.m.–5 p.m. one. I had to be in early to get through the financial press, so the latest I could afford to be at my office was by 8 a.m. I often had to remain after 5 p.m., sometimes till 7 p.m., to answer press calls and make press

statements. The job also involved weekend work, such as attending sponsorship events, cocktail parties, or there was the general socialising to be done just to keep in touch.

I lasted just over five months, when I decided I'd had enough. I could no longer handle the internal politics and the hours. However, if I had been doing a job I really loved, then my attitude would have been different. I felt that I would be far happier remaining at home and looking after my son and perhaps in time having another child, before it was too late, rather than keeping up the unequal battle.

I have been at home for over twelve months now and love it. I do not have a care in the world, no more pressures. And because he is now a toddler, he is very easy and my time is occupied doing things I want to do. I have taken up golf and play at least once a week. I go to college one day a week for dressmaking, and I have plenty to keep me occupied. I have no regrets about giving up work. In fact, I've given up on the idea of a career. Maybe when I have had my next child, and they are both older, I will consider running my own business – but that is now a long way off.

9 MANAGING WORK AND YOUR FAMILY: LEARNING ON THE JOB

Business women in smart suits, working long days, enjoying happy evenings. Photos of their young children on the desk in the office. Social successes, entertaining with home-cooked dinners. Loving husbands gently supporting their chosen career and parenting path. Bright, interesting children proud of their mothers' achievements in the outside world.

It's a relatively new image, but one that is growing fast as the ideal for all women to emulate. Perhaps the image also best draws out some of the conflicts women are currently experiencing. The conflicts are not necessarily those from within, but come from external sources. Any woman who has to compare herself against this supposedly easy-to-achieve ideal may well suffer from a sense of inadequacy and failure.

Then there are other external sources such as female colleagues, or relatives, who strongly disapprove of your working while you have young children. Male colleagues, or bosses, may simply not understand or approve, and they can make life very difficult for the woman already dealing with her own inner confusions.

But, as we've seen time and again in this book, women today – pioneering their way through hazardous terrain – are determined to achieve their personally held goals. They know and believe that they can and will be good parents and workers. Along the way, they have come to individual decisions about how much of an intrusion their children should be in the workplace; how much of an intrusion the workplace can be in home and family life.

Where some women proudly display the family portraits and loving pictures of little children, for example, others will have decided to keep such 'female' or personal artefacts well out of the way. Where some women, by way of another example, find that in a crisis they can bring the baby, or young child, into the office, others will refuse to entangle home and family in that way. They'll phone round all neighbouring nannies and relatives to help out in a crisis. But they will not expose their 'mother' self to their working colleagues.

'I felt exposed, having my home life on view in the office'

Ellen, managing director of a design company, has learned to be firm about not bringing her two young daughters into the office. With so many employees to worry about, her role at work is maternal enough – quite akin to running a family. To ensure time for her real family, she controls her outside-the-office activities and priorities.

By 6 p.m. or 6.30 p.m., she'll suddenly switch into a different gear, rushing off out of the building, usually frantically flagging down a taxi to be home by 7 p.m. She has cut down any after-hours socialising, which is common in her line of work. No breakfasts, or after-work drinks either. Equally, the intrusion of work into the home is controlled. Once home, she refuses to do any work while the girls are still up. Reading, or sketching, she saves for after 10 p.m:

> Only once did I bring the girls into the office with me, when their nanny was sick. But I wouldn't do it again. They loved it of course. But my daughters are extremely eccentric and I felt exposed, having my home life on view in the office. I am two different people.

FITTING CHILDREN INTO A BUSY WORK SCHEDULE

Those women who have entered exclusively male preserves, such as Philippa and Anne, with their senior management positions in computer companies, find that having children often eases tension with clients. Most men are happy to talk about their children too, particularly in a sales situation where the topic can quickly break the ice and make the woman appear more 'human'. Anne says:

> I actually found the fact I am a mother is an advantage, selling to men, as it gives them a chance to talk about their children, which they can't very often. The fact I'm a mother makes me seem more human too.
>
> Because I can't guarantee to be home before 7 p.m., I try and take my daughter to school in the mornings. If I'm home in time, I help with the bath. But it's flexible. My husband is often home before me. The school she attends is quite reasonable for working parents. They schedule Parents Day in the evening and Sports Day is on a Saturday. With the Christmas concert, we both knew well in advance, and took the day off work. Occasionally when my son is at a mother and toddler group, I take an early lunch hour and go along. As long as *I'm* comfortable with the situation and don't feel I'm cheating anyone, then we all stay happy.

PRIORITIES: HOURS AT WORK VERSUS HOURS WITH THE FAMILY

For some women, the number of hours expected of them, or that they still expect of themselves, slowly begins to change once they become mothers. Priorities can be visibly seen to shift – even for the most career-oriented of women. Very often, while the child in question is still a baby, the mother feels at ease leaving a nanny, or other childcare giver in charge all day. But, once the child grows older, learns to voice his or her complaints and demands, then the question of hours at work can become more vexed.

'Oh, he's so looking forward to your being here'

Sarah, the accountant and mother of two, who is now working in part-time consultancy rather than putting in those very long hours, says:

You just feel bad most of the time knowing, for example, that some of your colleagues start work at 7.30 a.m., and there you are scrabbling to be in by 9.30 a.m. Most of the men managers' wives don't work. In fact, discussions on those lines can get quite heated. Yet I really feel if I were to give up work, I'd go to seed. I certainly wouldn't be a brilliant mother either.

When I was working under such stress, I rarely took an hour for lunch, so I could leave earlier. Even when the pressure was very heavy at work, I did manage to leave for a carol concert and Sports Day, though it was extremely inconvenient.

One time sticks in my memory. My son was expecting me to watch a play in nursery school. I just couldn't get away from work. I rang the school but before I could get my excuse out, the teacher said, 'Oh, he's so looking forward to your being here.' I left work. What else could I have done? I couldn't let my little boy down like that. But would a man have made that decision?

A REVOLUTION IN PRIORITIES

Gillian, co-founder of a flourishing company, now mother of a 2½-year-old daughter, says:

I work far fewer hours now than I used to. In the evenings, I try to leave by 6–6.30 p.m., though that's always with difficulty. I certainly don't go to all the things I'm invited to. I imagine it will continue like that for ever. In fact, I fully expect things to get worse as my daughter gets older and can express the fact that she misses me.

I think I'm giving my career enough attention. Motherhood makes you reassess your priorities. And career is the first to go. There's been what I would call a revolution in priorities in my head. We women are spurred on by guilt at work anyway. But guilt over your child wins.

Larraine, the European MP, who puts in very long days with her work, but is also a highly committed mother to two children, says:

I'm always trying to work less hours, but I'm very responsible and serious about being a politician. So I'm desperate to cut down the hours, but also to do a good job. I work basically 9 to 5. Then I go home and look after the children. But I come back to my office from 7.30 p.m. to 11.30 p.m., to see what business is left to be dealt with.

What I do might be thought impossible. But in fact I'm around to take them to school in the mornings. At 5 p.m. I'm home to do baths, snacks and bedtime. And then I go back in to work again. I always go to school meetings and shows etc. I suppose in terms of naked ambition what I miss out on are those hours between 5 p.m. and 7 p.m. when the men are relaxing and chatting with each other. Informal networking. Also the other side of the coin is that I never read a book, nor do I exercise. I do the garden, that's about my only relaxation.

TRAVEL AND BUSINESS DEMANDS

Many of these same women find that being a professional, or in senior management, necessitates travel for work: to attend conferences, or have meetings with colleagues. Travel on business has always been seen as a perk to be fought over. But for the working mother it creates huge problems that can seem insurmountable.

Should she appear non-competitive and refuse to go away, for her child's sake? Should she compromise with her child's affections and go away for a shorter number of days and hope there are no major traumatising effects? Who needs the working mother more: her colleagues or her children?

Despite her influential position, Larraine has a surprising answer to the question about travel demands:

I just don't travel. I do all my work from the city we're based in. Though I make it look as though I get about the country. Recently, however, I went with a female colleague (who also has two small children) to the USA for a travel/study week. We both worked *all* the time. Gave ourselves no time for sightseeing. It was because of our guilt. We had to convince ourselves the trip was justified in term of work. But we both collapsed under the strain and longed to get home.

It did me a lot of good in terms of my work, to see how they approach women's issues in another country. And the children didn't seem to have missed me at all. We do have plenty of family around, and my husband was home every evening. It's just me, I feel I have to be around for them, though:

Most women do tend to juggle their compromises effectively; taking a few days off for conferences or sales meetings, making sure there is a relative or trusted friend to help out in the evenings, leaning more on their husbands to take over the helm at nights. As Ellen says, when she has to be away on business trips she find herself asking her husband why he can't get back from the office any earlier. She does it every evening.

Why do women worry so much? Children probably do not miss them, too critically, for a few days at a time. Husbands should and can perform a strong, primary nurturing role.

Anne travels quite extensively on short sales trips during the year:

My daughter works out where I've been to. I phone. I spend a lot on phone calls when I'm away. I do think companies should make provision for phone calls home, for men and for women. We're all part of families, and it's to a man's detriment that he disappears so much from his children's lives, too.

WHEN YOUR CHILD SHOWS ANGER AT YOUR GOING AWAY

Gillian has faced the very real and disturbing problems of travel and an upset child. She must make two or three major foreign buying trips a year for her company – each lasting a week or two. When her daughter was small, she took along the nanny, baby and her husband on one such trip – and it all worked well. But such events are expensive to set up, difficult to organise and only possible when the child is very small. Toddlers and school age children don't want to be dragged around after their mothers' career demands. They much prefer the routine of home. 'It's just a nightmare imagining paying for an extra room for the nanny every time,' says Gillian (and to work out plans to amuse them all day long in a strange country or city):

Once, because I had to go to Australia and couldn't afford to take our nanny with us, I hired a substitute there. That was a major feat of organisation to set up before we left.

So recently I went on a trip and left my daughter at home for ten days. I survived fine and assumed she did. But on my return, she was so angry that I then had to live through three months of behavioural problems. She was scratching me, hitting me, crying a lot, not sleeping at nights. We've just got over that. I don't know what I'll do when I have to go away next time.

One interesting line of thought dogs me, on this question of demands from work versus those from children: are there any working mothers who are foreign correspondents for television or newspapers? Do working mothers hold down executive sales positions that require travelling away from home a large percentage of the time? Would a woman, a mother, make such heavy compromises on her child's emotional life? Do women in those positions defer having children? Are we self-selecting our way out of competition for such lines of work?

JUST WHAT ARE MEN'S ATTITUDES TO WOMEN AT WORK?

Quite often in my interviews and talks with the women who participated in this book, I found we were debating the issue of working with men. Dealing with the men in our lives seems to be an unending concern for women whether it is in personal relationships, with regards to children, or as working women.

As we've seen in the last chapter, many women come face to face with the most difficult situations once they have become career-mothers. It was the sensitive nature of some of these topics that convinced me to keep all the stories 'fictional' by nature. If the women felt their identities were to be revealed, they would not have exposed their inner feeling in such a way. As it is, their comments build up to a very valid discussion for any group of men or women involved in the workplace.

Can men's attitudes to working mothers be expected to change? Or will they continue regardless, leaving women to adapt to the male ways and views? These questions are not going to be answered in the next few years, though there is a fascinating book on the subject by American author Kathryn Stechert, *The Credibility Gap:How to Understand the Men in Your Business Life – And Win by Your Own Rules* (Thorsons, 1988). Needless to say, it is never as easy as that title would suggest. In the meantime, women and mothers out there in the workforce are pioneering their newly held positions.

DO MEN THINK WORKING MOTHERS CAN REALLY HANDLE ALL THEIR RESPONSIBILITIES?

How many men, with wives at home caring for the house, cooking dinner, washing their clothes, worrying about the children's schools and health care, sincerely believe that a woman in the workforce, also handling all the above problems, can properly manage her time to the benefit of the company? Most working mothers will have come across the circumspect, cynical, ironic or downright critical comments from male colleagues. And women hold strong views on this topic.

Anne, for example, once produced a report on which she had to make changes. She says:

> I muttered something about not having the time, and my ears suddenly pricked up to notice the comment 'Oh, come on, you should be able to manage your time better than that'. My blood began to boil as I said, 'I have a husband, family and career to organise. *No one manages their time better than me.*'

Anne feels that, because of the constraints on them, women are a lot more efficient than men at work. For example, when she is planning a sales trip, she does not devote half a working day to organising it – but makes notes coming and going from work or in the evenings:

> Maybe I should do as the men. They waste so much time, and expect others to get involved in the time-wasting. Half a day on planning a trip. Then a secretary takes over and spends more time. Then memos go out and meetings are held all related to this one trip. He could have achieved the same in an hour or so of concentrated effort.

'A man would never say, "I'm leaving early to have a pint"'

Most women in senior positions, handling home and family life as well as business, describe working through lunch hours so they can leave earlier – to be home before the children's bedtime. And although they wonder whether such nose-down, hard-work tactics are beneficial in the long run, they are also waking up to the notion that, to be seen to succeed, thay are in fact going to have to copy certain male tactics.

Jane made the following observation about her future role and relationship with male colleagues:

> If you are in an office where the men are putting in fourteen-hour days, it is very hard to be seen to be competing when you go home at 5p.m. – even if you do work through the lunch hour. You are seen leaving early. There are simply so few role models in the corporate culture for working mothers today. We're still expected to compete with men on their own terms.
>
> A man would never say, 'I'm leaving early to have a pint.' We women tend to feel guilty about why we are leaving and let it be known we're going to pick up the children. We have to learn to keep our private life private. 'I'm going now' is the way to put it. No explanations. We've got to stop being apologetic.
>
> As I see it we're far better at time management skills anyway. Women's talents are grossly underestimated.

'Working mothers are generally highly motivated'

And Dee, mother of a 2-year-old son, who has managed to negotiate a reasonably balanced working week with her job in publishing, comments:

> Although we shouldn't expect employers to make any concessions to working mothers, at the same time there's no need to be apologetic because you have a child.
>
> Working mothers are generally highly motivated and a good investment for their company. It's reasonable to expect employers to be flexible, especially if the mother is prepared to be so. Employers seldom lose out because working mothers actually have a considerable commitment to their jobs.
>
> But the woman often expects too much from herself. If she's tired from lack of sleep, because the baby is teething, it is no less of a reason than having been out late and coming into the office with a hangover!

'The men here subtly put down women all the time'

Certain women express themselves even more deeply on the subject of dealing with male colleagues. Sue, the single mother and London solicitor, felt vunerable and hypersensitive about the attitudes of the men she worked with when she returned after maternity leave:

> It might sound a bit paranoid, but I felt I knew damn well what those men were thinking and saying about me. Here I was with an illegitimate baby, not married, and without even an official boyfriend as far as they were aware. They're a misogynist bunch here, under all their bonhomie. And underneath your obligatory smile you have to be very tough, if you're a woman. These men don't realise their own chauvinism, but they subtly put down women all the time. And they oppress them through their sexuality, by mockery, or mock-flattery, in all sorts of ways. Whether it comes from lust, envy or fear, I don't know, but it can hurt.
>
> I knew they were probably talking about me behind my back after I left early every day and never stayed around to socialise.

That can make them feel rejected, and they don't like it, and so
they have a go at you. I recognised all this and so my expectations
of these men, when I first returned to work, were minus zero.
After all, in their terms I had ballsed it up.

I never once brought the baby in or put a photo of him on my
desk. I didn't want to expose my son to any of those vibes. They
might have contaminated him. And he was my great pride and
joy: the one enormously positive thing in my life.

'A lot of men resent us for fear we are taking their jobs'

Two women who participated in this project were very
outspoken about the ways in which women managers can be
treated, whether they have children or not; ways that might
deter their promotion or ease of advancement. Their stories
are self-explanatory and not relevant to women in all lines of
business. But they are helpful to any woman trying to pick her
way through the often dangerous minefield of male-
dominated company hierarchies.

Kathy, mother of a 7-year-old boy, as a senior manager of a
building society, is in charge of two branches and nineteen
staff, plus four local agents. She started out in her career as a
cashier and has worked her way up with great success.
Because of the Equal Opportunities Act, the company was
forced to offer their women employees the opportunity to
train for management. But still, out of seventy managers in her
area, only six are women:

> I think a lot of men resent us for fear we are taking their jobs. Out
> of the six women only one other has a young child. My boss has
> said in front of me, 'A woman with children shouldn't be
> working'! I've been having another crisis with him this week.
>
> He is questioning my management decisions. I believe my
> management style is fair, but firm. I have had problems with a
> couple of members of staff and recently three of them left. So he
> has been looking quizzically at this. I see a situation and look at it
> from the management point of view and then try to persuade the
> staff around to my way of thinking. But my boss is seeing it as *my*
> problem.
>
> I work from a positive, optimistic point of view. He thinks I

make decisions emotionally, or too quickly. But he works very differently from me, and deep down I think he feels threatened. I've been here fifteen years, and have worked my way up. No one is going to tell me, 'You can't do it, Kathy.'

'Why can't you be more like a man?'

Philippa, in senior management with a multinational company, and mother of three children, is outspoken and visibly content with her dual role of career and motherhood; also she is quite aware of the deep vein of basic prejudice against women she has struck in senior management:

If there is a brick wall, you have to try to get around it and not through it. I do want to get on – not to be CEO [Chief Executive Officer] necessarily because my personal life is too important to me ever to give up everything for work. But at this point in my career, it is important that I make the next stage. This company has never yet let a woman through to that level. I'm pushing into an area where women have never been promoted in this country – though we're lagging behind the States and other European countries where there are women in far senior positions.

That's why it's bugging me so much. Here, I'm one of four senior managers out of 126. Seven or eight years ago, when I made it to the position of lady salesman, that was a *first*.

There is a lot of prejudice against women. It's the same old story really. To get on as fast and as far as a man you have to be twice as good. Appointments at a certain level are made as much on how you look, speak, present yourself and your image. It's to do with how you get on with the other chairmen. My theory is that senior management have to be 'comfortable' with you. There will always be two to four of you competing for the same position – so technically you know you're as good as they are.

But the big question is: have they ever seen a woman in the position you're going for? If not, they're going to have to make a conscious decision to put you in that position. And they're probably going to have to be *pushed* into it. It just won't happen as a general course. Why should they? It'll only make them 'uncomfortable'.

One of the comments I've been offered, by male colleagues – this is 'never tell a soul' stuff you hear after a bottle of wine – is that I should try to speak in a lower voice. Basically, to act more like a man. 'When we managers get together, we like to talk business and the City. We're not sure Philippa would *enjoy* that', was another one leaked to me. How do they imagine I get by in business now? Do I never talk about finance and the City? I handle many many very important clients – of course I know how to talk to them.

But, also one of the stepping stones to senior management is to work as a senior executive's administrative assistant. I overheard that the man in question might not feel comfortable with a 'dolly bird' as his assistant. I look young for my age, though I am 42. I have a bright, bubbly personality, so there is an element of 'Can we take this woman seriously?' in their attitude towards me.

I choose to wear my hair long most of the time. I'm fit. Most of the time I dress smartly and well to fit the corporate mould, and if I'm giving a presentation then I do tie my hair back. But I refuse to lose my femininity to fit their image.

When you're given advice, like the one about my voice, often you feel angry and follow it for a time. Until you realise you're making the situation worse by not being yourself. I've toned down my image somewhat. Now I speak less at meetings, although I make sure to make my presence known. Over the last two years, I've worked consciously on my image – to be aware of body language, etc. Office politics and games men play – that's another problem. I work hard, head down, and really haven't time for a lot of that nonsense. I'm very very honest, maybe too honest. It's all silly things. Like now I carry a fountain pen, especially if I'm participating in a meeting. It sounds awful, when I know a ball-point pen would work just as well. But these are the types of games men play

I hate myself for doing it. But you make a decision along the way – either you go flat out to be yourself and really don't care what happens, or you tread a more careful course, and fight for promotion – on *their* terms.

10 ALTERNATIVES TO FULL-TIME WORK OR FULL-TIME MOTHERHOOD

Many women feel they are in a quandary. Hardly a conversation with a working mother goes by before she'll begin to say, 'I would really prefer to be working part time, or for myself.' Or, 'Ideally I'd prefer to juggle work and family more.' But the conversation will then begin to take on characteristic overtones of doubt: 'I'm not in a position to take the drop in salary' or, 'I know that if once I went part time I'd be out of the promotional stakes. Work is important to me, I can't drop out now.'

Part-time work is not given significant status, nor does it usually carry rewarding salaries, or the security of pension and promotion. Unless you are highly talented, privileged or downright fortunate, it can be difficult to carve out that kind of work for yourself. Yet most men and women today pay lip-service to the belief that we should all be able to juggle work and family demands and needs. And the notion of the freedom inherent in running your own business seems very tempting to a majority of women.

Even Philippa, who is adamant about her ambition and determination to succeed within the multinational corporate world, says that if the right promotions don't come her way, within the next couple of years, she will move on. More than likely it will be to set up her own business rather than take a sideways step into another company.

Will part-time work ever be seen as a valuable contribution to society, and rewarded consequently? Will women who are mothers ever be granted the respect for the amount of work they actually put in, at the same time that they are compromising on promotion and advancement stakes? Or, as was noted in Chapter 2, is the tolerance for part-time work really tightening up rather than becoming more flexible?

MEN AND WOMEN SHOULD BOTH ASPIRE TO A 'MIXED PORTFOLIO'

Gillian, in her high-powered position, talked a lot about the stresses of keeping up the hours and about her deeply held fantasy to give up the full-time 'career' for what she called a more 'mixed portfolio':

> When you're a 'career woman', you get your status from your work. But after you have a baby, you become a mother, and it lessens the need to define yourself totally through career. That has helped me be more flexible; given me a view to wider horizons and change.
>
> My fantasy is to change jobs so I could have a more mixed portfolio. I'd really like to work three days in an office and the rest of the time be home-based either freelancing or acting as a consultant. I'd like to be part of the real world and have more time to be with my child. My values really have changed. At the end of the day, all the work I put in here is only for a business – which is not as real as having children.
>
> Really no one should just be stuck on a career ladder. You can get so jaded and boring. The pressures on working mothers are sometimes unbearable. You need time to nurture your best qualities and time for yourself.

HOLDING ON TO YOUR SENSE OF STATUS

Sarah, who has just taken a part-time consultancy position with her company, to escape the high-stress world of full-time career-motherhood, believes too many women lose their self-esteem when they work part time. Why? Because they see it as 'enjoying' themselves and consequently fail to take their own work with its true degree of seriousness:

I'm doing three days a week in the office, with proportionate holidays. My pension rights are under negotiation. My status with the mainstream company is suspended now, but if I go back for a year later on then it will revert.

I'm seriously contemplating studying for an MBA. I'll soon be 38, and I know it's a little unusual to begin such a course at my age but I'll be able to study part time, in the evenings, and then I'd have two options open: either to go back into mainline business such as merchant banking, in the finance world; or I could run my own consultancy business.

If I did start up my own business, I know I'd be working very hard. I'd be more committed and involved with the work. But I would be able to juggle my time to spend more with the children — all on my own terms.

One idea I've had is to buy a bigger house and open up a nursery for other working mothers! I know what their needs are at least. Now I'm working part time, I'm determined that this summer I will spend more time with my boys and make sure we have a good time.

WHY THE OBJECTIONS TO PART-TIME WORK?

In theory, at least, as women are becoming more valued in the workplace, companies will be able to make allowances for part-time work — with full-time status. As Sophia was quoted earlier, saying, 'Just because you work half a week, doesn't mean you only have half a brain'. Job flexibility, and the need to help women (or any parent) compromise over the amount of time devoted to office $v.$ family, will definitely continue to be major talking points during the coming decade.

In the meantime, women have to do some concentrated thinking and work, together, on just how they are going to achieve this ideal of part-time work with full-time status. As with any bargaining, or negotiation, the going seems that much tougher when you feel isolated, or the first one ever to have made such a suggestion.

I remember in my own working life very eagerly being interviewed for a full-time position on a newspaper. But all the way through the interview, the doubts were nagging away:

did I really want to commit all those hours, and heavy commuting, to this job? Was the position worth it, to eat away most of my waking hours? Would our family be as happy if I traded in my very being, the substance of my self, for the money and status involved?

I pondered asking the woman interviewer, a working mother herself, whether I could not take the job on a three-day week basis. I'm convinced I would have been as productive, as a feature writer on a weekly paper, for three days out of the week. But I was a coward. I didn't even bring up the topic. How do you present yourself at an interview for a new job, in heavy competition with plenty of other likely candidates, and say, 'I like the idea of working for you, but couldn't we just cut down the hours?'

The probable answer would be no. Most managers or supervisors are intent on keeping up the empire they have already built. To accept a three-day-a-week worker, in place of a five-day one, would cut down the size of her/his empire.

You may be seen as uncommitted, a poor risk, unlikely to be 100 per cent loyal to the company. Objections to the notion of part-time work are many and various: 'If I let you work part time, everyone will want to do the same'; 'It costs the company more to hire someone part time, because we'll probably need another part-timer to fill the gaps'; 'I like to see the people working for me at their desks. If we need you, there's no question of your not being there'. And deep down, the suspicion you are LAZY!

There are answers to most of these objections. Bargaining from a position already held in the company is probably the best one to be in. But you must be prepared. Write out your plan, consider the objections before you approach your boss or manager. And detail the strategy. Why it can and will work. Show your enthusiasm.

JOB-SHARING: AN IDEAL FOR PART-TIME WORK WITH STATUS

I want to be very careful not to sound too optimistic when referring to job-shares. Because I am able here to quote a couple of successful stories is not to imply that job-shares are easy to come by, common, or even likely to be accepted by all companies. As so many women have suggested they would appreciate this form of working, the ideal compromise, it would be unfair to build up too many hopes.

If the financial necessity of full-time work is not of vital importance, then working two to three days a week – sharing one position between two workers, your status and pay scales hopefully remaining proportionately the same – can help women successfully juggle the two major demands in their lives.

Why are there not more job-shares in practice? Largely the fault has to be laid at the door of unimaginative employers, unwilling to make concessions for women with children. Partly it is the fault of women not asking. But also involved is the logistical problem of the type of job and the necessity for two women who are colleagues also to be co-operative and trusting. Finally, more job-shares need to be seen to be working, to provide a good example for future decades of working mothers.

Here are two stories of job-shares in very different industries. They should provide encouragement and support for other women trying to embark on a similar line of problem-solving.

'The most notable reaction from men seems to be one of envy'

Megan is 44 and works in the legal department of a national company. Because she had always been a career-oriented person Megan did not think twice about returning to full-time work after the birth of her daughter two years ago. But, after nine months of full-time career-motherhood, she was so

stressed, exhausted and depressed, she was ready to resign.
There was no way of approaching the company to do her kind
of work, at such senior level, part time:

But then a female colleague in the department came and told me
she was thinking of getting pregnant. She knew how committed I
was to my job, but she could see what the stress was doing to me
and said, 'Let's do a job-share.' A few weeks later she came back
and told me she'd already become pregnant!

We worked out our strategy by doing a lot of research and we
built up a whole case. Then we took our senior manager out to
lunch, anticipating some difficulty. It had never been done before
at our level. But, to our surprise, he immediately said he thought it
was a good idea. We didn't even need our research. In effect, the
company was losing one job but avoiding losing two employees –
and we were both fortunate being in a specialised field which has
relatively few well-trained people.

We opted to share my colleague's job as it was at a lower level,
and would be easier to divide in two areas of responsibility. We
also felt we might face more hostility if she had had to be
promoted. We didn't want any bad feelings and we also wanted
this to succeed. We started the job-share before she went off on
maternity leave. I've been doing it on my own these past few
months – which has been a little fraught.

But the other significant part was our being able to *share* a
nursery place for the two children. I was very unhappy with the
nanny I'd employed which was causing part of the stress. I didn't
like my daughter having to spend so much time with her because I
was out all day. When I began inquiring about nurseries in the
City, I soon discovered there were none, but that there was one
about to be set up. I became involved with its foundation and am
on the committee.

We took the place from the day the nursery opened, even
though my friend's baby had only just been born. Even though we
are paying for days unused, we would far rather make that
financial commitment and be secure of the place. Travelling in to
work by tube when I was first bringing my daughter into the
nursery was quite a funny sight: me in my business suit and
briefcase, and my daughter in her buggy, clutching on to a rusk.
One City gent asked if she was a commodity dealer! Finally, I was
able to negotiate a car park space, as I just couldn't put her

through the rush hour journey every day. But she *adores* the nursery.

The job-share works out that we do two days one week, and three the next, with divided responsibilities. As we also share the nursery place, it's a great advantage as we can be flexible. If one of us has to work a different day, then the other just keeps her child home. We don't have separate nanny or childminder arrangements to work out.

My colleague and I have worked together for five years and were friends as well, which is probably important. We get along with both husbands as couples too. I was very lucky that she became pregnant so quickly.

We're also lucky, being in a well-paid industry, that both of us can afford to work just half a week. The contract says our hours are twenty-one, in theory. And we're both on half of her former salary, half the holiday and pension entitlement. The plan has caused some amusement among our colleagues but the most notable reaction from men seems to be one of *envy*. They'd love to be able to work half a week too.

Frankly, now I've got used to this way of life and drop in income, I'm not sure whether I'll ever want to go back full time. I may choose to do something personally more fulfilling, with less money. I'd like to do something with social significance and contribute to society rather than just helping make corporate profits.

'I have continuity, and the children see me as a real teacher'

Pat is in her early 40s, mother to two school-age children, and is currently working in a job-share as an art teacher in a secondary school. Before having children, she had taught for eight years in primary schools but felt she would rather be home for her children in their young years. So Pat resigned before her daughter was born:

I was ready for a break from full-time teaching and at the time did not foresee any problems in returning. I felt I ought to be at home with the baby in those days, and you either took the short maternity leave or resigned. Everything was thriving and I never thought it would be hard to get a similar position. But things have changed a lot in teaching.

I began as a supply teacher when my second child was about 3 years old. I had a neighbour to leave him with for the odd morning. But then the secondary schools got hold of my name and I was offered more work. I'd been to art school and have found teaching art at secondary level more fulfilling than at primary level. Also there wasn't much supply work in the junior schools.

I started by doing one day a week and became used to getting out of the house and back into teaching, although as a supply teacher I'd had to go back to the bottom of the pay scale. My husband also rather liked me working, the money helped out on things like cars and holidays. Though it wouldn't have been enough to hire proper childcare.

But then I was threatened with losing that one day. However, fortunately at the same time, the other art teacher was getting older and not wanting to give so much time. She suggested we did a job-share. It's actually *not* our county policy to allow this but the head was very keen and handed over the timetable and let us arrange it. The other art teacher and I talked it all over very carefully. We divided up the lessons and were left with one class to share between us, so she takes the major part of that.

The job-share is permanent – it's my job until I apply for another. It provides security for the school and for myself, because part-timers are the first to be dispensed with. To make it work, you have to find two people who can get on together. I can see, however, that if everyone in the school was job-sharing, it would be complicated. But we have been overconscientious about it. We overlap and we talk to each other about the classes every day. You must have continuity.

THE FEMALE ENTREPRENEUR

And then there are the women, with families, who set up in their own businesses. Generally, they have already dabbled in other forms of work, never finding the right balance of involvement and achievement; the right balance of hours for the office and hours for family.

Women with supportive husbands, women with unsupportive husbands, women on their own; somehow or other, whatever the obstacles, the entrepreneur-type battles on. Though, even for them, the idealised world of time for work and time for family may not be as easy to achieve as was imagined.

Helene, for example, runs her own software programming business and a software shop in a small city. She employs twelve staff and works with a partner. Helene has two young school-age children, is divorced and finds her commitments are a real uphill battle. There are times when the pressures of running the business and anxieties over money seem over-whelming, worse than the stress or pressures of a full-time job:

> I left school at 16, worked in a bank for a while and then as a secretary to an architect, but by 19 I had started my own business – in printing and advertising. I was married at 23, and my husband came in on that business as my partner. We bought run-down properties and did them up as another way of making money. At 27, I had my first child and the second baby came along two years later. I was soon bored staying at home with the children, so I went to college on day release for management studies. Then I began doing part-time work for a computer software firm.
>
> I was asked to work full time for them but I was not happy in the job. However, one of the programmers and myself decided to set up our own software company in partnership. At this point, I realised my husband was being less than useless. He wouldn't help me at home with the children or with the business. So we separated.
>
> Since then, during the last three years, running this company and the new shop, I have found it's all been quite a struggle. In this rather rural area, I have a real problem finding reliable childcare. I'm running a business and cannot be home for them every day after school. Really I need a wife at home. But I am highly self-motivated, and on the positive side I do get a lot of job satisfaction.

'I was besotted with the work and my own success'

By comparison, Jennifer's road to setting up and running her own business was trouble-free and easy. Now aged 58, Jennifer was a domesticated 'housewife' for fifteen years,

bringing up her four children – until they reached the ages of
5, 7, 11 and 13. Formerly, she had worked as a dancer, a
model and as a secretary. There was never any career plan. But
now it was time to find a line of work that suited her:

> I didn't enjoy being at home with the children all those years. I
> couldn't wait to get out and be my own person instead of being a
> servant to the family. I wasn't sure what I wanted to do, but I felt
> that by experiment I would find something. So I began working for
> an employment agency and discovered I was very good at that kind
> of work. But, when I wouldn't agree to work full-time hours they
> sacked me and I went into business on my own – that was fifteen
> years ago. Now I run the most successful small business in this area.
>
> For years, I was besotted with the work and my own success.
> I've been lucky in that my husband has been very supportive of
> my efforts and so has my family. I'd never trained for any
> profession but learned about business management along the
> way: about insurance, the law, PR, advertising – which is a great
> all-round training.
>
> I would say, if a woman is over 40, it might be best to open her
> own business – rather than try to get in on a full-time career with a
> company that may not recognise her talents. You have to take
> risks when you haven't been trained, but you come in with a fresh
> eye which can be better. My business has brought me self-
> satisfaction, status and recognition. I've made money too, but I
> refused to let the business grow too big, preferring to remain in
> control of all sides.

But now for some stories of women who have survived
juggling what has been described as the 'patchwork' of career
and self-fulfilment that has always been so typically female.
For some, a career that will fit around motherhood begins
with part-time work and moves into running one's own
business. For others, there are periods of self-employment,
freelance work, charity obligations ... any number of
variations upon a theme.

PART-TIME WORK: PART-TIME PROBLEMS?

Sometimes working for oneself is far and away the best compromise. You don't have to be a high-flying business-woman making millions. Many working mothers are content to bring in an income from self-employment based at home. But the freelancer or self-employed faces her own set of problems: anxieties over money, insecure status, and maybe lack of recognition from any other adult.

So just how do the part-time, the self-employed, or the woman with her own small business find this way of life works out? There are, of course, a variety of different experiences and involvements. My own, as I described in Chapter 1, has always been to work for myself. Any doubts are superseded by the fear that going into a full-time, out-of-the-house job/career would detract from our family life.

Other doubts are supplanted by the knowledge that an office-based job would need to pay considerably more to enable me to pay a childcare substitute. Yet further doubts are superseded by the fact that as long as I can continue to work this way, carve out my own niche for status, respect and recognition, I'm content to accept the freedom and mobility self-employment affords as my own form of compromise.

'I'd had a fantasy that my home would be a serene workplace'

Most women who are working in some alternative fashion have made the decision based on the fact they want to be around more hours of the working day for their children. They do not feel right entrusting their child's total care to someone else. They feel guilty (or loving) enough to believe their place is meant to be with the child for at least an equal amount of time as with one's work.

Thirty-five-year-old Lucy, formerly a secretary/office manager, describes going freelance as part of a master-plan to work at home while caring for the baby:

I started my own business as a freelance technical writer about a year before becoming pregnant. What a crazy pipe dream it all was! I soon discovered that I couldn't string two consecutive technical words together, much less form a complete sentence, while at home looking after the baby. I had to get away from him in order to focus and concentrate on technical data.

I'd had a fantasy that my home would be a serene workplace; a fantasy which my son shattered when he came screaming out of my womb. Then, too, you have to take into account colleagues' or clients' prejudices. One of my freelance writing accounts, a consultant, dropped me like a hot potato when he learned of my pregnancy. It was just as well, as I needed to cut back my workload by about 30 per cent anyway, just to compensate for the unexpected exhaustion from round-the-clock feeding.

When my son was about 3 months old, I arranged to use a free desk in the office of one client for whom I did a lot of work. I needed to get away from my baby's screams in order to tolerate them when I got back home. The office was a peaceful retreat to which I could escape and compose myself. No matter how busy and hectic the office report work and deadlines, it was serene compared to the colicky scene at home!

In the six years since then, my job has grown into that of a full-scale office manager. The man I work for has added ten employees and I now have a full-time secretary, word-processing specialist and a receptionist. I run the financial affairs of the office, full time really, but on part-time hours – and pay.

'I make good use of my time and am very productive'

Annette, the mother of two sons, a consultant psycho-therapist, faces up to the inherent conflicts in her chosen way of life every part-time working day.

When I had my first son, I was 33, and although I planned to continue doing my research one day a week, I felt ready to stop for a while because I found looking after the baby utterly exhausting. I was very positive in my attitude to being a 'real' mother and breastfed for the first year. But then quite a few of those fantasies were shattered as I found myself isolated from other women, and that conversations with other mothers were not adequate.

So, after six months, I started going back to the clinic on a one-day-a-week basis, and I left the baby with the woman next door. It was the most important day in the week for me, when I felt I had a real purpose. I could have lunch with colleagues and talk to other adults. I felt very strongly that I wanted to look after my baby but not to be at home all day, every day.

I carried on with my research and was very productive. Because my time was finite, I made good use of it. While the baby slept in the mornings, I'd be writing my thesis for an hour and a half. It's a tremendous discipline. I completed my Master's degree and gradually increased the amount of work, so I was going in two or three days a week – now using a daily nanny. Then I became pregnant again at 36 and miscarried. A year later, I had a second successful pregnancy. During this time we had moved because of my husband's job but I was able to land myself a position at another very good clinic.

I took on six sessions or twenty-one hours a week of work. It was more than I wanted with a 9-month old baby, but I grabbed the opportunity. Along with my other work, I wrote and edited a book in the evenings when they had gone to bed.

Now my children are older, sometimes I feel I'm always running against the clock. A considerable part of me wants to pick up the children from school, yet I would also love to be able to devote those hourse from 3 to 6 p.m. either to work or to building up other contacts. Just for myself really.

I'm interested now in a different position which would be full time. If I go for it, it would mean not only the longer hours but meetings everywhere, working breakfasts, all the management responsibilities. It's at once a challenge and a dilemma. I just don't yet know if I will apply.

'Life seems too short to fill with work'

Gail's children are now 22 and 19, either married or away at university. For all her working/motherhood life Gail has juggled jobs, part-time positions, a typical 'patchwork' career. First, having trained as an infants' teacher she taught part time. She then travelled with her husband's job, and on their return home began working part time as a secretary for her husband:

Then an old schoolfriend asked me to help her run a new business venture – a second-hand shop selling on a commission basis everything from clothes to antiques. This has been successful and twelve years later we are still very much in business. I only work two days a week at the moment, though it has been as much as three and a half days in the past. At the moment I fit the rest of my life around it. Throughout all of this my husband has been in well-paid employment, so it has never been necessary for me to work to support us, and I realise I am fortunate.

Four years ago, I was elected to the national committee of a women's organisation, and I was editor of their newspaper for the first two years. This was another new experience for me, but one I was very keen to have and that I particularly enjoyed. It took up most of the rest of the week and, because it's a job done from home, most of my evenings too. For the last two years I have been the national organiser, which takes up even more time and carries a lot of responsibility. But now I am just giving up that involvement and I know it is going to leave a big hole in my life – as I am not really needed in the home any more.

However, full-time employment does not really appeal to me. Life seems too short to fill with work, and there are so many things I still want to do, both for myself and with my husband now that we are alone again. Ideally, I would like a part-time job that involves some of my interests: mainly health, diet, relaxation, exercise, education and alternative medicine. I have thought of trying to teach relaxation to young children, thus combining at least two of my interests. Or taking courses to turn some of my interests into areas of expertise. I am aware that in the last four years, I have gained many skills: administration, printing, editing, meeting and dealing with people, that could make me quite useful to an employer.

'Someone has to be there for the doctor, or dancing lessons'

Even a generation ago, if they worked, mothers would have felt obliged to compromise their ambitions and career-objectives to fit around family – particularly around a husband's career demands. Deirdre, a trained GP and now consultant psychiatrist, aged 58, mother of six grown children, describes her own quite remarkable achievements like this:

I have only worked part time for the past twenty-four years because of family commitments, and because my husband's work meant that practical help from him was never available. As a GP, his evening surgery finishes about 8.30 p.m., and he has night and weekend duties too.

Working part time is always more than the sessions allowed or paid for. Women also have to work harder in order to avoid criticism of being overinvolved at home.

I had to leave general practice as the workload is far too unpredictable for someone with a young family. Someone had to be free to take the children to the doctor, dentist, to dancing classes, etc. At one point, though, I knew I was working more hours than my husband's part-time female partner, for one-third of her salary, having been qualified for twenty years longer!

'My husband has been envious of me – as he's stuck on the career treadmill'

Gail, whom we met earlier, who experienced a variety of ways that women tend to work (apart from full time) – following a traditional pattern of the educated and well-married woman for whom financial concerns have never been a great problem – had this to say about today's women's options and choices:

My husband has been envious in the past when he has been on the career treadmill, and I have been able to take life at a different pace. He is now in a job that is giving him similar scope, and it is turning out to be as enjoyable and rewarding as he imagined.

I do think that women are in danger of spoiling the situation for themselves by taking on too much, or being forced into taking on too much. We never seem to know when to say no. It is definitely something we should learn.

The pattern of most women's lives consists of a period of career after school with either training or university. Marriage, or a stable relationship, may come along any time in her 20s and 30s, but children will probably not feature in her life until she has worked for at least five to ten years.

Motherhood will almost certainly be a great shock to her system, no matter how she has planned for it, and even if she imagined herself devoting the next few years of her life to the children, she may still find she wants to be involved outside the home and baby interests. Other women will choose to return to work after maternity leave, either for financial reasons or because their career development is very important to them.

But, in a working world still predominantly male-oriented, women seem to have to be twice as good as men before being recognised, appointed or promoted. We've certainly all been educated to believe career is of equal importance to mothering, but maybe too much emphasis is laid on getting back to work.

A few years ago, women were made to feel guilty if they weren't fulfilled in the home and needed some outside stimulation in the form of a job. Now the opposite is true. Quality of life is very important too, and it may be that some women (and their families) might actually be happier with a lower standard of living, but more time to enjoy their lives, to be themselves instead of always someone else's mother, wife or employee. Now everyone seems to be rushing from one activity to the next with hardly any time to draw breath.

It is good to be busy and usefully occupied, but some women seem to be pushing themselves a bit too hard with all the demands on their time. One wonders what advantages they have achieved over their predecessors, who were worn out by the sheer amount of household work they did, without the benefit of the labour-saving devices that have freed us – for what? – more work!

11 CAN MARRIAGE SURVIVE CAREER/MOTHERHOOD?

The superwoman myth has adversely affected all women, so today we are convinced we should be able to perform at peak. The collective image to achieve is that of the slim, elegant, well-dressed, and perfectly manicured, successful lawyer or businesswoman who, at the end of the day, goes home to the support and care of a loving husband and to play with her charming baby.

Just imagine – if we feel threatened by this image of perfection imposed upon women – how today's man must surely find himself on the defensive from his expected 'superman' role. Gone from our collective consciousness of 'ideal' is macho man, swinging from branches, controlling his woman and family; enjoying, in subtle ways only he understands, their complete loving dependence on him – and subordination to his every whim.

Today's man has to be supportive of his career wife, able and willing to cook a perfect meal at the end of both their working days, prepared not only to change the odd nappy, but to take an equal part in night-time feeds, evening babysitting (while his wife may be out to important meetings), and stay at home with baby when she/he or the nanny is ill.

Superwoman will never be heard to brag about a partner who doesn't quite make the rating on that score card.

Now we no longer feel the need to parade a wealthy husband who has enabled us to remain at home, pampered and bored. The man to show off is the one who underwrites our working life and motherhood.

Failure today is to be a woman who cannot say (with the

correct syrupy voice), 'My husband is *so* supportive, I don't know where I'd be without him.'

Needless to say, the story is seldom that picture-perfect. Few fairy-tale princes are that good, but then, what is supportive to one woman might be a bully to the next. The only truth to come to terms with here is that if women, in relation to motherhood and careers, are undergoing major transitions, so are men in relation to women and their careers.

The inspiring part is that so many women are intent on handling this transition with or without the support of the men in their lives. Which, it doesn't take a psychiatrist or marriage therapist to interpret, has led us swiftly into our new area of conflict and complexity. The problem in sum for women today is often basically about men, marriage and partnership.

THE LUCKY ONES HAVE A GENUINELY SUPPORTIVE HUSBAND

Those women lucky enough to be able to say (without a flutter of hesitation), 'My husband is *so* supportive', talk of situations of genuine sharing. As Philippa describes, the enormous difference in the tone of her two marriages in itself depicts a change in attitudes. The second time around, she and her husband discuss all the childcare issues; they phone each other during the afternoon to see who will be able to get home first for their 2-year-old son. They both hold equally demanding, well-paying and stimulating jobs. Philippa speaks with the determination of someone who has seen a previous marriage dissolve precisely because that man was locked in traditional attitudes: 'I wouldn't have had our third child if I didn't really believe he would support me in my career *and* motherhood. My need for a child in itself wasn't so great,' she admits.

The couple makes sure there is time for at least one evening out together a week, and once or twice a year for holidays alone – without any of the children. They know that marriages cannot survive alone on tight, pressing schedules and hurried phone calls about childcare.

Naomi, who is 36 with a 2-year-old son and a career in ethnography, is determined that her husband live up to his early promise of being supportive – an equal partner:

> I expect him to be continually supportive. Some men are very keen at the beginning, with a new baby, but it can slacken off. I have several outside commitments, as well as my full-time job. I work with Black arts groups in the evenings. Frankly, it's nice to get out of the house and be involved. My husband spends a lot of time with our son, and we share the responsibility of taking him to and collecting him from the childminder.
>
> But I have noticed that my husband expects and needs a lot of vocal gratitude. If he were a wife he wouldn't expect anything like the amount of 'thank you's. Why should I have to say 'Thank you for looking after our son this evening'? Is it really my job, and he's just helping me out? Or is it maybe the male way of seeing things? But he'll still make comments like, 'Look what I did *for* you', as though he were really only filling in on my duties.

Maryanne, who recently returned to full-time work on a newspaper, after nearly ten years freelancing from home while her children were small, has also had the support of a husband who did his equal share of playground duty. Now they are both working, he continues to share their childcare needs:

> My husband and I work out our professional commitments so that one of us can be there to give the kids dinner, or whatever. We sit down and work these things out *beforehand*, so that there's no last minute discussion in loud voices about who should have done what.

But what about those husbands who are not so co-operative, who do not fit the decor and plans of today's working mother? Very often women who have compromised their working life, as mothers, discover they are still viewed as 'traditional' mothers – expected to look after the children.

I can well recall, in my own experience, how different it was asking for a husband's help during those times I was genuinely working outside the home, full time. When I had to leave before school time, he was very happy to fill in on those duties. But, the story was not the same for my at-home based working. Somehow, in the mind of the man, women are there to fulfil those 'motherly' duties first, and to work second. Even though her salary is of equal importance in the smooth running of the home. If we're suffering from confusions over roles, then, rest assured, the men are in a worse fix!

JUST AN OLD-FASHIONED MAN

Many of the women I spoke to, particularly those in the 40 plus age bracket, had knowingly married traditional, old-fashioned men, with rigid attitudes to a woman's place. During those long years of marriage, very often it is the woman who first makes changes in her life. When she decided to continue with her career, as well as having children, she found not so much a supportive, co-operative man, but in many ways an enemy.

Yet, for reasons best known to themselves, these women often stick lovingly by their partners, despite all the odds. In the cases I am quoting next, both women interestingly are doctors. I would hazard several guesses about the consequent situations. Do women who wish to become doctors choose old-fashioned husbands? Is it that in medicine, being an early field with which women become seriously involved, we find career-mothers among their group before any others?

'It irritates me when he sits around in the evenings'

Ruth, at 41, mother of an 18-month-old son, is a senior medical officer in local government who has been married to another doctor for sixteen years. Her husband, although delighted with the baby, considers the childcare her total responsibility:

My husband spends a lot less time with our son than I do. I think he'll find it easier when the boy is older and can talk to him. What I notice is that my husband has been successful with his career and can cope with most things – with the one exception: a child whom he can't control and doesn't know what to do with. No, he's not a modern father in the sense of changing nappies and getting up in the night. He never did do a great deal to help in the house and I didn't really expect any change, though it irritates me when he sits around in the evenings and says *I* need a rest.

He feels it's important that I continue working now, though originally he imagined I'd give up my position when I had a child. It's a conflict men go through, I think, of wanting an intellectual wife and having all the domestic chores done for them too. You develop a compromise over these things during the years, however. I've accepted the situation.

'He never once ironed a shirt or did the shopping'

Deirdre, the psychiatrist formerly trained as a GP, now 58 and mother to six grown children, says of marriage:

Young women should discuss careers and finances before marriage. And they should make sure to marry someone who will support their ambitions. My husband has had no idea what six children and part-time work entailed. For example, he never ironed a shirt, took anything to the cleaners, did any shopping or cooking, until two years ago when I began working full time. I used to cook lunch for eight in a preset oven, when I was commuting to London for training, and then I'd cook again when I got home so we'd have a freshly prepared supper.

Deep down I'm also resentful about my husband's insistence on the financial benefit of work rather than seeing the pluses for myself of building up a career. For example, the car and domestic help had to be paid for out of my income, and if I wasn't going to make enough money he wouldn't let me take the job. I also feel resentful about his lack of emotional and practical support. I still feel tearful when I see a father pushing a pram – my husband never did.

'The one person who suffered from my stress was my husband'

In other cases, it is the stress involved in the woman's working life and attitudes that leads to marital conflict. Megan believes that when she was undergoing her high-stress nine months of full-time work after maternity leave – before the job-share was worked out – the person who suffered most was her husband: 'I took it out on him. I think I resented the way he only had to cope with his job, not with everything else.'

'I couldn't neglect my son and I couldn't neglect my work'

In some marriages that we watch from outside, we can believe it's the husband's fault when the relationship hits a high watermark of tension because the man apparently feels overly threatened by his wife's ambition or success. In other cases, the wife seems to be causing the problems, with an overcommitment to work or because she has succumbed to stress.

Kathy, building society manager and mother of a 7-year-old boy, describes a situation in her marriage that led them finally to counselling:

I had taken on extra responsibility managing two offices and I was bringing work home with me too. I was aggravated all the time and didn't know what to do about it. There was a lot of backstabbing going on in the office, and I felt the need to put more time in at work to compensate for my having had the child.

What I couldn't cope with was running and organising a home, work and my *husband's* needs. I couldn't neglect my son and I couldn't neglect my work. So it was our marriage that suffered. It wasn't ever a conscious decision, but it happened. We just stopped talking and really had no contact with each other, except for arguing, for weeks on end. We thought we were talking to each other, but it was all being expressed in slanging matches.

In the end, I knew that either we'd have to seek help or we'd break up. Initially, he refused to go along to counselling. He said it was *my* problem. I went along to the first session on my own, and immediately began to see what was happening. I was told we needed a long talk, to list down all our complaints about each other and give them an airing. It was very painful. My husband did not find it at all easy to open up, but in the end he came along to one of the sessions and even he found that just talking in front of that third party was very useful.

The building society industry is very male-dominated and I was the only female manager in a region of forty men at my level. What he'd been feeling was jealousy of the other men when I went away on training courses; and resentment that I passed the buck in the sense that, whenever I went away, he had to bear the brunt of looking after our son. He felt as though he was left to cope with things while I was off having a nice time!

A lot of the problem was that we were both exhausted. He had job pressures too, and we weren't giving each other any emotional support. Once we started talking, things began to improve. It wasn't a very nice period, but it was worth going through.

WHOSE CAREER IS THE MOST IMPORTANT?

The my career versus your career, enemies at bay, attitude can be a problem in any two-career couple, and is clearly aggravated by the presence of a child or children. Many couples, quite capable of behaving and acting like equals – before a baby comes along – discover that along with the birth arrive all sorts of inner pressures and needs that are not easily met. New tensions arise within the marriage that they certainly did not expect.

In real, practical terms, the issue basically is concerned with whose job, or career, is worth losing a night's sleep, or who can take time off to take the child to the doctor? I remember reading a book by an American writer about the complex topic of working mothers and their guilt-quotient. The author described her own involvement in the topic with a story about the time her children went down with chicken pox. I was interested because, like me, she worked as a freelance writer, and was able to juggle time for work with time for children – helped by a daily babysitter who was, however, not altogether reliable.

The author had been able to set up a major piece of work

for herself that included a number of interviews and a few days travelling to meet those people. This project had been arranged long in advance. A schedule was set up with narrow gaps between the interviews.

The morning she was supposed to leave, her little boy had a raging temperature, and there appeared before her eyes the dreaded chicken pox. In terror, she telephoned the babysitter who refused to come because she had never had the disease herself. The author was stumped. She did not feel capable of asking a neighbour or grandparent to expose themselves to chicken pox, either. Her husband had already left for work. What did she do? She cancelled the whole trip and all those prearranged interviews.

I have to say that reading that particular story and the way this woman handled the situation made me very angry. My own husband was certainly not perfect, but my immediate response would have been to lift up that phone and say, 'You *have* to get home. I have a plane to catch in under an hour, our son/daughter has chicken pox. I cannot possibly give up this commission, annoy all those people who are lined up for interviews.'

What was most startling, in her recording of events, was that she made no mention of even trying to ask the husband.

THE ANGER CAN UNDERMINE ANY MUTUAL SUPPORT

Too many women carry the whole burden of guilt for their children's care on their own shoulders. Dr Elisabeth Herz, consultant psychiatrist and gynaecologist at the George Washington University Medical Center, Washington DC, is skilled in treating career-mother patients who have been referred to her for emotionally based problems:

A kind of angry interaction grows up between a couple over this question of whose career is most important, that undermines any mutual support. Both parties need to be very clear in their conversations with each other how they will arrange, or rearrange priorities once they have a child. Women must be realistic in the role they assume with regards to childcare, so the marriage doesn't come to the point where each partner has expectations that are *not* being fulfilled by the other.

Women who come to see Elisabeth Herz frequently present themselves with stress-related gynaecological problems. Or they arrive on their own in an attempt to sort themselves out, recognising they are not as happy as they expected to be – now they are mothers.

Indeed, Dr Herz now believes we should be extending the ante-natal services to preconception counselling on psychological concepts such as: 'What do I expect motherhood to be like?' 'What do I expect my husband to be like as a father?' so that couples can talk over some of these issues before ever having a child. There are times when a couple really should not have a child:

You have to work on some of these expectations and come to a realistic and negotiated compromise. To expect 50–50 sharing in child raising is a myth that will only lead to unhappiness. Yet, at the same time, too many mothers force their husbands away from the baby, not allowing him to build up a close, intimate, trusting relationship with the child on his own terms.

It can all end up as a power struggle and if one *wins* the relationship in the end loses. The most couples should expect is a situation where neither is entirely happy, but they can live with the situation and agree on the compromises. That should be one of the basic philosophies of marriage to start with.

EMOTIONAL AND STRESS-RELATED SYMPTOMS

Women who come to see Elisabeth Herz with non-specific problems may complain of feeling uneasy, or depressed, or talk of marital tension. The husband may have sent her along, seeing it as her problem alone. Emotional stress-related symptoms would include discomfort with intercourse. There may be a physiological cause, such as vaginitis, but more than likely it is that the lack of sexual arousal derives from emotional tension.

Such functioning is triggered by the brain, and if a woman is feeling angry or resentful with her husband because he is not being supportive nor helping with the baby, then she will not be easily aroused for intercourse. Indeed, marital tension is a very effective way of turning off the libido!

But other women may also experience vague undefined complaints that they cannot pin down: abdominal pains, fatigue, headaches or lack of energy. Any of which might come from anaemia, caused by blood loss after birth, but they may also be the symptoms of a body crying out from emotional disturbances.

SINGLE PARENTS MAY EXPERIENCE LESS OF THIS TYPE OF CONFLICT

Despite the obvious stresses and strains of being a single mother – handling her career, keeping up the emotional stability of child and self while undergoing all the hardships of that period immediately after birth, such as lack of sleep and fears of her own inadequacy as a mother – the single parent at least does not have to worry about the father's equally urgent needs.

Dee, who works for a publishing house and raises her 2-year-old son herself, had this to say about marriages of friends and colleagues she has witnessed:

> Having no experience of marriage, I can see, however, that the impact of a child on the relationships of various friends has been dramatic. There's no doubt that the ultimate responsibility for the day to day care of the child always seems to rest finally with the mother. You can just about get away with social and emotional differences between men and women until the children arrive, then it will polarise all sorts of unreconciled problems. Not necessarily insurmountable problems, but there often has to be a major renegotiation of the terms of the marriage or relationship before they can progress.

It seems to be somewhat easier if this is a very traditional relationship and their expectations are therefore well defined. Men are generally a conventional bunch. But at the end of the day, it always seems to be the woman left 'holding the baby'.

In some ways parenting alone removes enormous areas of conflict, although it's not easier in a multitude of other ways. I would prefer to be sharing all my parenting – the good times as well as the bad!

'It's important not to dump the burdens on your husband'

Annette, at 41, mother of two school-age boys and a part-time consultant therapist, speaks from the experience of a long-standing marriage, and with the thoughtfulness of a woman who works as a counsellor herself:

My husband and I have a good friendship, but there is always tension because it is difficult to create enough space for *our* relationship. Finding the time and the space, that's the problem. When the boys were younger we had a live-in nanny for a time, and that was one of the best times of my life. I had the freedom to be able to phone him during the day and rush into town so we could meet after work, go to the cinema or out for dinner. We were free to function as a *couple*.

Now, even though the boys are older, we haven't reached that same point of freedom again yet. Our eldest is 12 and we can't very well hire a teenage sitter to watch them so we can go to a film. In fact, I still feel very trapped. And I know this leads to tension between us as a couple – to a lot of built-up resentments.

I do resent that he doesn't have to do it all, take on the burden of guilt and the emotional pressures. I feel jealous that he can just ring up and say he'll be late home if he needs to meet someone after work, whereas I have to book time from him in advance. It's quite a straitjacket I work under – I wouldn't even have time or space for a lover if I wanted one!

On the other hand, I do think it's important for your marriage to survive that you don't dump your burdens on the other partner. We have to learn ways of talking to each other – so it doesn't come out as an accusatory 'Will you be here on Thursday at 8 p.m. so I can go to...?' That creates tensions and there is little room to work those out together.

SUCCESSFUL WOMAN ... LOUSY MARRIAGE?

Many many marriages of successful women do, indeed, come unglued along the way. I found the book *Successful Women, Angry Men*, by Bebe Moore Campbell (Arrow, 1988) quite enlightening on the reasons behind such break-ups, or breakdowns, of relationships. One woman I spoke to at length said that when she attends network meetings of the top and most powerful women in the country, the most notable topic of conversation is about divorce, husbands who have walked out and run off with the secretary, or the problems of finding new partners for already successful women.

Many many successful women, as we have seen in this book, also have successful, loving and continuous relationships with one partner. Sophia, in her own right a millionaire from the company she and her husband founded together, spoke very frankly about problems that happened recently in her marriage, which might well prove helpful if you are finding shifting sand – rather than solid rock – is now the basis of your relationship:

'He was quite genuinely threatened by me'

Three years ago, when we were first doing really well, we decided to hire a PR company and, as I was a rather visible woman heading a company, it was agreed that I would be the 'publicity' spokesperson. After all, it was fashionable for women to be successful and we knew we'd attract more publicity that way. I was a bit wary at first, having always accepted my role as my husband's partner, mother to our two children, and was really quite happy being slightly in the background – the devoted, loyal compassionate woman.

Well, Bob went off his head when I started to become a public figure. This totally normal man became very bitter and peculiar. He was difficult about everything, muttering about other couples we knew with little asides such as, 'She really has him under control' and 'He's not *allowed* to do anything'. He started drinking more and generally making my life miserable.

I really do think that just as men have feelings about the work ethic – that money and status are the only measure of their success – they also feel they have to provide and be the boss at home. He was quite genuinely threatened by my taking a more exposed position.

When we first met, I got pregnant immediately and dropped out of 'proper' working to the more secondary role of caring for our castle and my king. I was the doer. He was the creative one with the bright business mind. I was practical, quietly going about things behind the scenes.

What neither of us had taken into account was the change going on in *me*. I'd always had a rather low opinion of my own ability. And, at the time it's happening, you don't realise you're changing. But I was no longer quite so dependent on him.

It all came to a head the day Bob told me I could either have my marriage or my career. I was devastated. I'd only ever wanted to be married to him. We're both strong personalities and probably deserve each other. But I decided at that point that no one would pull the rug from under *my* feet.

My career was completely tied up with him, the family, our house, etc. The so-called choice he was giving me was totally unfair. What was he expecting me to do? He really thought I'd opt to return to the kitchen sink! So I said I'd hang on to the job, thank you. I moved out of our house into the office down the road. Emotionally, though, I was heartbroken. But I was not going to give in to him completely.

One of the ironies of the situation, clear to me, was that I could only be so successful in this company because we ran it together – I was in a position to exercise ultimate flexitime, work when it was suitable to me and to our children. If we were to split up, and I would have to find another job, I would be much more tied to office hours and expectations.

Although we both had a lot of thinking and inner searching to do before we were able to come back together, I know that I have become a lot stronger from that experience. Our marriage will never be what it was again for me. He destroyed so much trust that I'd naively placed in him. But I have learned to temper my personality. Maybe I reacted defensively and aggressively towards him because I wasn't sure enough of myself.

Similar situations seem to be happening all round among our friends. I know a lot of forceful women and threatened men. Some couples are still together – with problems. Some are no longer together. And some of the men have severe mental problems because their self-esteem has been so wounded.

But I do think we women have to decide for ourselves what we want and stick to it. In my case, I want to devote a lot of my time to family – but equally I want to devote time and energy to work. And I'll arrange things that way. I want a family, and a job, and to be loved. That's the balance. There are compromises to be made along the way – but that's my decision. I don't feel I've compromised too unfairly.

12 IS THERE A BALANCE WE CAN ACHIEVE BETWEEN WORK AND FAMILY?

All the women who participated in this book found there was one question nagging away at the back of their minds. However hard they tried to rationalise their current lifestyles, there was still the worrying 'How can I try to achieve the best of all worlds — working with sufficient commitment to be successful, without causing any harm to my child?'

Strange though it may be, in the last three decades we have witnessed many major social revolutions, yet are still plagued by an overriding fear of 'What makes a good mother?'

The minute any woman gives birth, she becomes part of a collective consciousness, realising there is in reality no way she can live up to society's ideal of 'the Good Mother'. Along with birth comes not only a baby and all the concurrent responsibilities, but also lifelong guilt. For women, that is.

TODAY'S IMAGE OF A 'GOOD MOTHER' HAS CHANGED

Far from freeing women of the burden of living up to a 'good mother' image, all the social revolutions have merely left us with a new set of criteria to be filled. Peter Moss, senior research officer at the Thomas Coram Research Unit and co-author of *New Mothers at Work: Employment and Child-care* (Unwin Paperbacks, London, 1988), emphasises that the burden still falls *solely* on the mother to create of her child a 'worthwhile and fully-realised adult': 'Today's "good" mother is expected ... to help (her children) develop to their fullest potential in all ways. The responsibility should the child fail to achieve this potential rests with the mother.'

Fathers do take some blame for a less than wonderful child-turning-into-adult; but never with such heartfelt criticism as is meted out to the 'mother who worked'.

But there is a balance that can be struck between ours and our children's inner needs and demands. Women are practising this form of balance every day. Women are also talking about such issues. When the topic is broadened out to include the men, some very angry debates can ensue.

ARE WORKING MOTHERS HANDICAPPED RACERS?

In her book, *The Equality Trap: Why Women Are in Trouble at Home and at Work* (New York, Simon & Schuster, 1988), American lawyer Mary Ann Mason argues that equality has proved to be a trap for women: 'The real revolution is an economic one that requires a woman to work the whole of her adult life, taking little or no time out for the demands of motherhood.'

Ms Mason's thesis is that women are trying desperately hard to keep up their act both at home and at work, with little support. Because we wanted so badly to join the male workforce, we accepted our admission on their terms. Which means we have to work like men, put in the same kind of hours; then go home to cook, clean and care for the children as 'good mothers': 'Then they discover that the male working world has not changed to accommodate the needs of mothers. An executive or lawyer is not expected to leave promptly at five to pick up a child at a day care centre, or to stay home with a sick baby.'

Taking the argument further, she underlines that the concepts of equal rights and equal pay, for example, do not challenge the fundamental structure of the economy or the role of the government: 'Asking to be treated as men are treated is a fundamentally conservative position that asks for no special support from the government or special consideration from employers for working mothers … In short, equality is a trap for women.'

WHAT WORRIES CAREER-MOTHERS?

They worry about their children, of course. Will their insistence on working ultimately affect the child's future life? As Gillian, mother of a 2½-year-old daughter and co-founder of a small company, who works very long hours, says:

> I'd like to be able to look back on myself in twenty years and see just how the children of working mothers have turned out. We still really don't know the answers, do we? I think we all ought to be looking more into guilt, competing guilts, conflicting loyalties and the way women endlessly try to please – their male colleagues at work, their husbands, their other relatives … even their children.

Anne, in senior sales management with a computer firm, mother of 5- and 2-year-olds, who mostly feels very content with her dual role and juggled life, felt the word 'apprehensive' best sums up her attitude:

> I'm probably giving a disproportionate amount of time right now to my company. But this stage of my career is very important. I work hard, never take lunch, get home tired, talk a little to the children and to my husband, watch some TV and fall asleep. There is something missing in there!
> There are times, too, when it all seems overwhelming. Of course, I keep masses of lists. The only way to deal with the problems is to work on things one by one. Slowly, as you begin to check them off the list, they begin to resolve and come together. If I ever tried to face up to *everything*, altogether, at the same time, that's when I feel I might go crazy!

SO WHAT IS A 'GOOD MOTHER'?

In their latest report, published in New York as *Know Your Child: An Authoritative Guide for Today's Parents* (New York, Basic Books, 1987), a team of child psychiatrists has tackled just this issue. Drs Stella Chess and Alexander Thomas have been running a thirty-year longitudinal study on how children's personalities and behaviour patterns develop from infancy to adulthood. They have given unique thought to the particular socialising concept that makes all women take on this burden once they become mothers.

Chess and Thomas describe the route taken by attitudes towards maternal employment from the time of Abram Kardiner, a prominent psychoanalyst at Columbia University, who wrote in 1954:

> My own experience with working mothers indicates once again that the predominant emotion they feel is guilt. I have no choice but to believe this guilt is the price exacted for maternal neglect in the interest of self-enhancement.

Go out to work, if you dare, after reading that one!

Even noted paediatricians Drs Spock and Brazelton were caught up in this 'dim view of the mother's working unless it was absolutely necessary'. Spock included his discussion of working mothers under 'special problems', until his 1976 revision, declaring that these children were in danger of growing up maladjusted. Before 1976, Spock was emphatic that it made no sense for a mother to work and pay someone else 'to do a poorer job of bringing up her children'.

And, in 1969, Dr T. Berry Brazelton was arguing that 'two mothers are not as good as one in the first crucial years. It is better for an infant to have one figure to relate to, to understand, to absorb, as he sorts out his own reactions to the world.'

WHY WERE WE SO AFRAID OF WORKING MOTHERS?

This unrelieved picture of the harm done to children if their mothers worked outside the home had arisen from the influential works of people like Freud, and John Bowlby whose *Maternal Care and Mental Health* (1951) concluded that mother love in infancy and childhood is indispensable for mental health.

Chess's and Thomas's own circumspect view of these long-held and still last-ditch attitudes is summed up in the words of philosopher Jerome Kagan (1984):

> Every society needs some transcendental theme to which citizens can be loyal. In the past, God, the beauty and utility of knowledge, and the sanctity of faithful romantic love were amongst the most sacred themes in our society. Unfortunately, the facts of modern life have made it difficult for many to remain loyal to these ideas. The sacredness of the parent–infant bond may be one of the last unsullied beliefs.

MOTHER'S ROLE-SATISFACTION IS JUST AS IMPORTANT

In a later section Drs Chess and Thomas, who have studied minutely the thoughts and behaviour of a range of children, now turned adults, have this to say about the changing attitudes we are witnessing today in our Western societies, towards maternal employment:

> We have now a veritable mountain of evidence on maternal employment outside the home. If any subject has been thoroughly researched within the past twenty-five years by child psychologists, psychiatrists and paediatricians, this one has. The data are abundant, and the conclusion is clearcut: the children of mothers working outside the home are not harmed if a satisfactory caregiver or caregivers are provided.

Of course, the issue for the child will be different if the

substitute caregiver is inadequate. But the child will also not prosper with a mother who stays at home if she is an inadequate caregiver. Child abuse can occur in a bad childcare centre; it can also occur, perhaps much more frequently, with disturbed parents at home. The research evidence also strongly suggests that it is not the mother's employment or non-employment outside the home that is significant for the child and herself, but rather her role satisfaction or dissatisfaction.

In 1976, Dr Spock's revised *Baby and Child Care* was published in which he acknowledged (in quite revolutionary fashion) his earlier prejudices. Spock stated:

> Both parents have an equal right to a career if they want one ... and an equal obligation to share in the care of their child ... If the mother has resolved her guilt and doubts, her children will not only accept but be proud of her working.

More recently, as an example of how the tide is turning, an article in the *New York Times* Sunday Magazine (9 September 1984) by Anita Shreve, titled 'The Working Mother as Role Model', took an absolutely positive stance. This article was later published as part of her book, *Remaking Motherhood: How Working Mothers Are Shaping Our Children's Future* (New York, Ballantine, 1987). Says Ms Shreve:

> Studies suggest that independent and achieving mothers engender similar qualities in their daughters, and that these daughters have higher career aspirations and greater self-esteem than daughters of non-working mothers. Child specialists also believe that as more children grow up in the families of working mothers, both boys and girls will find it easier to balance their masculine and feminine characteristics than their parents did.

HOW ARE THE CHILDREN TAKING TO YOUR WORKING?

To return to that pressing question, some of the women from this admittedly limited study revealed a few of their concerns, or feelings about the state of their children's emotions. Some were not afraid to share with me some of the honest and quirky (maybe difficult) comments that have arisen. For example, Anne said of her children that they are very independent and don't seem to be suffering by both parents working:

> I'm very close to my daughter and not so close to my younger son. Though when he was little I was the only one who could stop him crying. Now, I have to say, he's closer to Nanny than he is to me. He tends to call us all Mummy – myself, Nanny and my husband. My husband once mentioned this to his colleagues, and they looked at him very strangely! I suppose it must sound awful to another man whose wife does not work. As though I had abandoned them.

Ellen, managing director of a business, mother of two daughters aged 12 and 8, is also very aware of things her children will say:

> As much as you try and tell them, your working life is inexplicable. They don't really understand what you do between 9 a.m. and 6 p.m. As they get older they tell you how much they miss you, and let you know they deeply resent your going off. 'If only you could be a housewife, Mummy,' they've said to me!
>
> But when they ask me why I work, I do say because I love it, and because it's great fun. In addition, I mention it means we can have nicer holidays, and they can go to decent schools, etc. Your children must know you work, because you *want* to. Particularly as daughters, I want them to have a role model of women doing something they *enjoy*. My mother worked intermittently, but never in a 9–5 job.
>
> Also, timing works against you. During the day, you work very hard and intensely, then go home where you have to try to pick up the threads of their lives in a few minutes. It doesn't quite meld. Finding a way to get into their lives in a couple of hours in the evenings can be a trial. Holidays are very important as at last our timing can be in sync – there's time for real emotional work.

WORKING TO IMPROVE SELF-IMAGE FOR BOTH SONS AND DAUGHTERS

Indeed mothers of sons and daughters all had positive things to say about creating valid role models for the future generation. Nancy, who juggles her part-time college work with some at-home childcare, comments about her three sons:

> I look forward to them becoming more independent and acquiring skills to take care of themselves so they do their own laundry, make their own meals. I do feel the responsibility of rearing tomorrow's men. I want them to understand it's not just Mummy's job; that they don't get up at the end of the meal and leave me to the chores.

Maryanne, newly returned to full-time work on a newspaper after years as a freelance, says of her children:

> They understand that spiritually I need to work, and that financially, to support our lifestyle and the house we all love, it is also a necessity to have my income. They see that some of their friends' mothers don't have jobs. But while occasionally they say they wish it were true of me, usually they are realistic – and proud of what I do. My husband and I also share our work with the kids. Many parents seem to think that this is adults' stuff, but the children are suprisingly knowledgeable about our fields, and I believe that draws a family together.

'They resented being brought up by au pairs'

Deirdre, the 58-year-old doctor and mother to six grown children, who struggled through retraining to become a consultant psychiatrist, looks back and says:

> It's all too complex to sum up. I'm aware of my children's resentment at being brought up by au pairs, although I was only out of the house for four half-days a week, until the youngest was 15, and then only six half-days. And I feel totally to blame for any emotional difficulties in the children.

On the other hand, I am thrilled at my children's successes: two have Oxford degrees, one from Cambridge, one from London University, and the other two are still undergraduates. I'm also delighted that they are doing things other than medicine, such as history of art and Chinese theatre! For myself right now, I'd love to be living in London with a full-time research and teaching post. And I want to see all the children happily settled and have lots of grandchildren!

'Could I ever go back full time? That's a very big question'

For Megan, who changed from full time to a job-share nine months after her return to work, the balance seems almost perfect; especially with the full-time nursery place that is shared by the two children of the job-share:

> She used to cry when I left her at home with the nanny. but now with her going to the nursery, I feel guilty the days I stay home! She'd rather be there. When we drive in, and turn the corner to the nursery, she can't wait to get out of the car.
> I've refused to look ahead and worry about what will happen with the job-share. Because I'm 42, it's unlikely I'll have another child. But my colleague may want to have more. Maybe in three or four years, when my daughter is in school, I'll go back full time, but maybe I won't. And if I did go back to full-time work, frankly it wouldn't be to this company. I'd rather do something for less money that was personally more fulfilling. Could I go back full time? That's a very big question.

Sarah, currently doing a three-day week part-time consultancy position in accountancy, after being full time for five years following her first baby, is now thrilled to be giving some more time to her growing children:

> Our family times have always been wonderfully warm, apart from the usual fights and complaints. I'm happy to be taking this summer to give them some more of my time — we'll visit grandparents and do things together. I'd like to put more credit in their bank of happy memories . . . I think it will give them strength as they get older. They've only ever known me as a full-time

working mother, so now it really is a golden opportunity to be able to do this for them. I'm not saying I'm going to be as available for the rest of their young lives!

WHAT IS YOUR EMOTIONAL STATE REGARDING CAREER/MOTHERHOOD?

For my study, one of the questions I asked concerned the emotional state today's working mother finds in herself. The question I posed was: 'How would you best sum up your emotional state regarding your career/motherhood role now? Euphoric, content, satisfactory, exhilarated, energised, exhausted, frustrated, confused, depressed, angry, resentful, complex, scared? You don't have to pick just one!' (For the rest of the questionnaire see Appendix.)

The answers were fascinating, the majority tending to choose a mixture of descriptions showing some exhaustion, a lot of confusion and complexity, interspersed by some exhilaration and contentment.

Here, some of the women you have been reading about through the book describe their feelings – on the question of balance between work and family demands, and on guilt and confusion.

'Happy – but torn between conflicting obligations'

Lucy, whom we met in the previous chapter, had tried working freelance at home as a technical writer but found her colicky baby's personality too much of a threat to creative work. Now she works part-time hours (doing a full-time job) as an office manager for a busy architect. She struggles with many of the conflicts we have been discussing throughout the book:

I have never been happier in my life. But I've never felt so torn between conflicting obligations. It is good to feel needed, it is dreadful to feel you are failing those who need you. For example, when my son had chicken pox, I rose to the occasion, cancelled everything, and stayed home to nurse him for a week. He had one of the happiest weeks of his life. A month later I am still untangling the chaos that resulted at the office.

Jennifer, a newly qualified staff nurse working sometimes difficult shifts, loves her new-found career after years previously as a secretary:

> What I want to be able to say is, 'I really love this job but I would prefer to work either part time of four ten hour days so that I can have more time with my family.' Also I have dreams of saying to my bosses, 'Be understanding because, at this point in my life, my family comes first.'
>
> I feel that my children are only going to be around (as children) for a short time. I brought them into this world and I owe them the best upbringing that I can give them. They need guidance in order to turn into responsible adults.
>
> When I became pregnant, I thought I was going to be superwoman. I would have it all – motherhood, marriage and career. How naive I was! We women really do have it all – ulcers, heart disease, etc. Before my first child was born, I was determined to return to full-time work. The child would have to fit into my life, I thought.
>
> I was not prepared for the feeling (maternal instinct?) that was awakened in me. I grew to believe then that my children and husband are the most important aspects of my life. My job (career) will always be second. Nursing is a demanding role at best. When I'm at the hospital, I work hard. But when I leave, my job has to stay there.

'Space "just for me"'

Annie is one of those women who have experienced a patchwork career following their husbands around. She works in a secretarial capacity but enjoys getting out and away from domestic life:

> My emotional state would best be described as exhausted. Frustration is there too as I like to do things well, and sometimes I can't do them as well as I would like to.

Annie also mentioned a much-used phrase for what she would like in her life:

> I have always been a highly energetic, gregarious type, but my most pervasive fantasy at the moment – and it has been the same for a couple of years – is to have space *just for me*. By this I mean complete solitude for a while and, if we could afford it, I would love to rent a small flat somewhere that either of us could go to have to have time to be alone.

'I wish I wasn't tired and sex could be spontaneous again'

Many women made reference to the fact that marriage, their love life or sex life seem to be the first victims of the stress and exhaustion experienced when juggling motherhood and career. Sally, a 28-year-old who works in advertising, commented:

> A mother's day is very long. The work day, by comparison, seems very short. When people ask me what is wrong, I tell them I have been tired for three years, since the day I gave birth to my first child. Other than that, I am very happy being able to have the opportunity of both working full time and being a mother. But I wish I were not tired all the time, and that my husband and I could have sex spontaneously. You have to be prepared to have your life, especially the time you are used to sharing with your husband alone, turned upside down.

'I used to think I could do it all'

Angela has just recently given up working, as the demands of her three children and the vagaries of a patchwork career have not made her working life an easy path:

> I used to think that I could do it all, and in all modesty I think I've done – kept up – with more home/work responsibilities than many others. I've never had complaints about my work, never been fired, reprimanded or warned. But it's so *gruelling* a pace. Now I just think I can't do it all, at the same time, or without help.

My emotions are complex: angry, resentful, proud of myself, self-reliant, fearful. I want my daughter to have better resources and more independence. I adore my husband but the truth is he still makes far more money than I ever have.

There's a lot I'd like to say to my boss or colleagues, along the lines of: 'Follow me for my childbearing years – *feel* pregnant, *experience* three C-section deliveries, struggle through the post-natal time, and go back to work *before* you're ready. Leave jobs as I did to take the maternity leave you really want. Run your household – squeezing in doctor appointments, groceries, errands – and still be on time, completing projects on deadline.

Try to summon up some sexual response to your mate when you're so tired you just want to weep. Remember birthdays, parent conferences, cancel *your* work day for a sick child. Breastfeed at work, pump milk instead of going to lunch, try not to be angry and bitter at the difficulty of arranging childcare, and the lack of nurseries. Add up the money you spend to accommodate your working – wondering if it all balances out. And let me say, *I could have told you so*!

'I care about my career, but not as the answer to my life'

There is always the love of your children to keep you going, which is one thing we do not give up when we continue working into motherhood. Rosemary, a part-time office manager, feels quite adamant in her view on the necessary balance:

I was not prepared for the total love and attachment I feel for my children. I didn't know once you became a mother there was no going back, that you always have someone's welfare in mind. It affects everything you do in life.

I care about my career but not as the 'answer' to my life. Neither my children nor my career need to be everything now – they share very well instead. I find that nice. I enjoy throwing myself into whichever one I'm focusing more on at the time. Previously, I never thought motherhood would rate anywhere near my career.

Right now I feel satisfied with the mothering I am doing. I want no more and no less. I feel I benefit from working part time. I would not be doing so well if I worked full time, nor if I were home full time. Everyone has to find what works best for them. All I can count on is that the children will grow older and get on with their lives.

I like being there for them. But I like doing for myself mentally as well. They have a better life, I can assure you, when I am mentally fulfilled and happy.

13 SURVIVAL STRATEGIES FOR CAREER-MOTHERS

Survival for the woman with a challenging career, or for any woman returning to work shortly after having a baby, will probably mean less how she copes with the workplace, colleagues and bosses, and more how she handles her own emotions. The survival strategies I want to talk about here are not tips to help you get to the top, but some deeply felt advice that may help when everything seems to be falling apart around you.

As some readers of this book may already be aware, previously I wrote *The New Mother Syndrome* (London, Unwin Paperbacks, 1987), which is devoted to research and enlightenment of the topic of postnatal depression. It is more than likely, if you are a woman who has enjoyed some degree of success and/or competence in her working life, you've already decided you will never be affected by postnatal depression (PND). How wrong you are!

As I wrote in that book:

Surely successful women are not special cases for suffering PND? You may believe, as do so many of the women in question *before* they become mothers, that these women are all set to be the new superwomen of our society. They are used to achievement, organising, and dealing with people and situations. They have status in the working world, probably can negotiate for time off or easier working hours more successfully than a woman with a less flexible job; even better, they have money and can afford good childcare, thereby alleviating some of the guilt. What could they possibly have to complain about?

I then quoted a 36-year-old woman with a fine career in banking, who had been married for eight years before having a child, and who had felt she was ready for anything: 'We think we can handle anything because we're older and have advanced in our careers. Yet when we take home a tiny infant and realise the baby is totally dependent on us for everything, it's just overwhelming,' said Suzanne.

Although *The New Mother Syndrome* initially investigated the hormonal or biochemical causes of PND (and looked into the historic reasons why its treatment and recognition has been left behind), by far the greater part of the book analysed the psychological effects of motherhood. These are as true for the busy working or career mother as they are for the more traditional home-based mother.

WHAT ARE THE EMOTIONAL STRESSORS?

Let me list a few of them and see if they ring bells with you: a sense of *inadequacy* that you are not performing at peak, mainly as a mother; a crisis in your *identity* which may be even stronger now you are back at work: you are not the same woman who rushed off to give birth, narrowly escaping landing the baby on the office carpet. If you're not the same person, then just who are you? Emotionally you are much more complex now, torn with conflicting loyalties, worried by your guilt, and much more prone to tears than you've ever been before.

You might be feeling frustrated or even angry towards yourself, that you seem to be making heavy weather out of what is meant to be an idyllic period in your life. There is resentment, as we have read often in previous chapters, towards your husband who does not have to face up to all these issues; resentment maybe to other women around you, and particularly towards male colleagues who don't, won't, or cannot understand. Worse, you feel their implied criticism for what you are struggling so hard to achieve. Their wives stayed at home with their babies. Therefore, by extension of logic (that oh – so male – preserve), you must be wrong.

At the same time, these are male colleagues with whom you have to deal, work with, co-operate, maybe live with every working day. Deep down, you know they have no rights to be prying into your personal life, and you resent that. Do you criticise the way they get home so late every evening and miss seeing their own children? Do you criticise their overconscientious use of the local wine bar every evening?

You're a woman in command, in charge of her life – and somehow you've got to battle to keep up your self-esteem.

Being in control, finishing each day with a sense of competence, or pleasure at a job well done, feeling proud of yourself for the double life you are leading – these are all important aspects of the emotional feedback you should be receiving.

But, if you're feeling tired, exhausted, emotionally fatigued – the battle is going to be all that much harder. So do get as much sleep as possible.

GUILT – THE GREAT ROBBER OF SLEEP

Sarah, who has described her own level of exhaustion and how the stress involved in keeping up with ever-increasing hours and demands at work have finally led her to take a part-time post instead, also mentioned that she had not had a good night's sleep for the past five years. Her two children, now aged 5 and 2, are both poor sleepers and Sarah gets up to comfort them, to change nappies, to bring juice to their little beds. Why doesn't she ask her husband to take over? What about the nanny?

But the nanny goes home at the end of the working day. Her husband travels a lot and besides, says Sarah, because she's out all day working, she has always felt her children have greater need of her in the evenings and nights. Even as she spoke, Sarah could hear the unwritten suggestion. Her guilt about being away from them is the driving force that gets her up two or three times a night. I said laughingly:

If you stayed at home all day with those children, and had no exciting career to steal you away, you'd let them cry it out at night. You wouldn't be able to bear hearing their voices again. And you wouldn't be chastising yourself that you're not being a 'good' mother, either.

WORKING MOTHER GUILT

Working mothers tend to overload themselves with obligations and responsibilities just because of that guilt. It's easy advice to give – and hard to live out in our own lives – but there has to be a way of finding a happy compromise. Obviously, you don't want to feel you are neglecting your baby or young child, but equally, it is very easy for a woman to neglect herself. She literally allows her self to be devoured, absorbed, consumed by the child – to compensate for that twenty-four-hour mothering she thinks she should be giving.

FROM 'PERFECT' PREGNANCY TO ... WHAT?

Since the publication of *The New Mother Syndrome*, both here and in the US, I have often given talks either to groups of women or to professionals about the complex nature of PND. One of my favourite points is to discuss the issue of 'perfection' that seems to be plaguing Western, highly educated, sophisticated, twentieth-century women. Forget about having it all; we expect to have, do and accomplish it 'all' to perfection. Whether this drive comes from the fact most of us will only have one or two children – so we demand a heightened experience from our attempts – or whether it is all part of today's driven, success-oriented world that we live in, whatever the cause, we expect, somehow instinctively as part of our birthright, ultimate happiness and ultimate success from our experience of motherhood. And, most importantly, from ourselves.

HOW TO ENJOY THE 'BIG EXPERIENCE'

When I was seven months pregnant with my first child, I finally set sail for my new life in New York. Because I was beyond the acceptable state for flying in aeroplanes, and because I felt this was a momentous 'voyage out' – a journey that metaphorically spelled out the enormous changes in my life – I went in style on the QE2. Needless to say, the fare was costly. Also, I must add, it was at the back of my mind that it was likely to be the one and only time I sailed on the QE2 in my whole life.

I was aware, therefore, from the moment of finding my tiny cabin, and exploring the great and magnificent ship, that I had just under five days to enjoy this experience. Just under five days to ensure my trip was memorable, fun, something to tell the grandchildren about. What if I hated it (which at first sight seemed quite probable as I gazed dispiritedly around at the blue-rinse crowd on board)? What if I *failed* (note my italics) to enjoy myself? What if this did not prove to be one of the 'big' experiences of my life? I panicked for the first few hours, having laden myself with all these expectations to be met, extra stresses and pressures, on five ordinary days of my life.

That's rather similar to the way we treat our experience of motherhood these days, don't you think? It just has to be memorable, wonderful, satisfying, fulfilling, all encompassing; just the biggest and best thing we've ever done in life. And, of course, along with that expectation are the fears. What if we *fail*? What if we don't get ultimate enjoyment out of the experience? There's no going back. Just as I couldn't make the ship turn round to start my five days off again.

We plunge into the experience of motherhood from the very beginning with zeal and determination. Most working women today take their pregnancies seriously. We eat the right foods. We go to the proper exercise classes. We buy the 'dress-for-pregnant-executive-success' clothes. One friend in New York went to prenatal classes called 'Dynamic Pregnancy'. I can recall groaning for her sake. 'OK, so your pregnancy might be dynamic, but early motherhood is far from that. Doldrumatic may be more the word,' I wanted to say.

So there we all are, rushing around exercising our right to a perfect pregnancy; then we expect (even demand) a perfect labour and birth experience. If we are delivered by forceps or Caesarean section many women feel again that either they have failed or they have been failed – in their expectation of perfection. Next we turn to breastfeeding and again expect ourselves to be perfect earth mothers. And baby will be just a little darling who magically knows where to latch on to, and what to do.

CAN THERE BE 'PERFECT MOTHERHOOD'?

And then . . .? Then we go home and discover there is no such thing as 'perfect motherhood'. The experience may be inspirational and dramatic; possibly even just the most wonderful thing that has ever happened to us. But, again, it might not be. We've never had to cope before with unbroken sleep, an unbroken rhythm during the day of taking care of someone else's physical and emotional needs. The pressures and stresses of office or professional life appear easy by comparison.

Maybe we yearn to escape – and wish we'd taken off less time for maternity leave. But then we are instantly plagued with guilt for such a thought. No 'perfect mother' thinks that way. Maternity leave is our right – and again, we expect, and demand, to enjoy it.

Maybe we regret returning to work so soon, because really we're exhausted, and feel confused, and just don't know what has hit us. And we're feeling a new kind of emotion, as though the umbilical cord was never properly cut. Yes, we want to get back to work, to the adult world of papers, reports, conferences and appointments. But is the baby really going to be all right with the woman we just hired – in whom we're about to place all our trust?

How will you ever manage to get out of the house – on your first day back at work – looking smart and shipshape, with a tidy briefcase actually holding all the correct papers and not filled with nappy liners? You're very aware you're not some young secretary who can giggle her day at work away. Yours is a position of responsibility, and none of your colleagues will want to listen to the fact you got hardly any sleep last night and forgot to get the only other suit that fits you back from the cleaners.

That's why I talk about survival. I do think we should all be doing our best to help each other through what can be very difficult times. Women do each other a disservice by continuing to pretend everything is perfect, that they are perfect working mothers, when really they're just as confused as you.

SUPPORT NETWORKS

In the Resource section, at the back of the book, I have listed all the many and various working women's networks that exist. Maybe you are already a member of one of the groups. Maybe you just never find the time to go to meetings any more. After all, once you've arrived home in the evening after work, have played with baby and helped put her or him to bed, there isn't much freedom for taking in evening meetings.

Many women continue to meet up with same group through the National Childbirth Trust (NCT) with whom they shared antenatal classes and discussions. This can be a valuable resource – to get together, even if it is only once a month, maybe with your babies, to talk about good times, bad times and problems. But, the likelihood is, unless you live in a very special area, that you will be outnumbered by the home-based mothers, and the group meetings, unfortunately, may only help further undermine your self-esteem.

Some cities and larger towns do now have specific NCT Working Mother groups which are obviously the most beneficial. What I want to suggest, if there is not one in your area, or if you know there are several other working mothers within your company, is that you set up a group yourself.

Some busy professional women find the best time for such a group meeting is in the lunch hour. Most professional women dash for trains and cars, to take them back to the suburban home they bought because they were starting a family, by the early evening. It's best to use that time when you're all together in the city. It can also be far easier to allow yourself the time out during a lunch hour than in the evening.

Book a room in a restaurant, treat yourself to a decent outing, have a break from the stressful routine of always eating a sandwich at your desk, and over a glass of wine share your feelings and fears with like-minded women.

If the company you work for is small, and there are few women who have babies of similar age, there is no reason why working mothers with children of any age cannot meet together. If your concern is getting enough sleep, and someone else's is what to do about after-school hours, the support and help offered by a group of women is always worthwhile. The same holds true for part-time workers, or for the self-employed working mother. Just place an advertisement locally and see how many responses you receive. Most working mothers are as desperate to meet someone else of their own kind.

Professional working mother groups can be a most effective way of networking. You may find yourself meeting women at all levels of business, maybe from different or related companies. Your meetings can develop to take in some issues specifically related to the workplace. You may expand to the point where you hire professional speakers. You can even take the opportunity to sell off your second-hand baby equipment and clothes!

And don't worry about male jeers as you scurry off to your lunchtime meetings. No, they cannot come along. (Let the fathers set up their own groups.) And, remember that deep down they're only jealous of the fact that you can blend these two sides of your life so successfully. That you have the involvement and feedback with and from your child.

Because, despite all your fears, you really are having it all. You are fulfilling your emotional, spiritual and intellectual sides, at one and the same time. Keep up the good work! And good luck.

APPENDIX

1 March 1988

Dear Colleague

For a major project on working mothers and their careers, I would really appreciate the time and energy involved (and we all know those two commodities are in short supply) if you would answer some of the following questions. I don't mind if you scribble in pen in the margins, type a thesis, talk on to a tape – or arrange to speak to me personally. I just know there is a lot of emotion and information that has not yet been exposed. And now is the time to bring our own particular problems out of the closet.

Don't worry about being quoted personally. Anyone's material eventually used for publication will run with a fictional name. And I will send you a copy of the section for your approval.

Thinking along the lines of *You, Your Career, Your Child* (as a working project-title) would you tell me be about:

(1) Age, education, career history, marital status, etc.

(2) Were you able to plan the pregnancy beforehand, to fit in with a career plan? Was this plan something you had in mind from girlhood? Do you wish now you had approached things in a different way?

(3) Were there any specific problems regarding your position at work, once you announced the pregnancy?

(4) Did your male, or female, colleagues treat you differently either once pregnant, or since motherhood?

(5) Have you changed the number of hours you devote to work since motherhood? Has your attitude to work affected your ability – or how others see your ability?

(6) Do you think you have been overlooked for promotion, since motherhood?

(7) Are you giving as much attention to your career, right now, as ideally you would like to?

(8) Are you giving as much attention to your child, and/or other members of the family, as ideally you would like to?

(9) Do you feel appreciated at work, or at home, for what you are doing?

(10) How do you fit in travel (or not) for work, conferences, special meetings, that encroach on time with your child?

(11) What would you most love to say to your boss or colleagues given the chance for complete honesty?

(12) How long a break did you take off after/around the birth? Was this ideal?

(13) If you returned to work after more than six months, were you able to take up your former position and salary level? Did you change careers? If so, were interviews a problem?

(14) Has being a working mother affected most your previously held view of marriage, motherhood, or your career?

(15) How would you best sum up your emotional state regarding your career/motherhood role now? Euphoric, content, satisfactory, exhilarated, energized, exhausted, frustrated, confused, depressed, angry, resentful, complex, scared? (You don't have to pick just one!)

(16) What is your most pervasive fantasy?

(17) Any comments or advice to other women?

My previous book, *The New Mother Syndrome*, by Carol Dix (New York: Doubleday, 1985, Pocket-Books, 1988; London: Unwin Hyman, 1986, 1987) was about coping with postnatal (postpartum) stress and depression. Writing and researching that book led me into a campaign to help other women deal with an often difficult time after childbirth.

Then, the response to a simple quesionnaire like this was so revealing and exciting, that I hope to tap again into a well of unexpressed feelings. Now, I very much look forward to your replies/response to this new project.

With my very best wishes,
Carol Dix

RESOURCES

THE CHILDCARE CRISIS: A FOOTNOTE

Who will look after the children when mothers continue to work, rather than dropping out of the workforce for whatever number of years? Feminists have been raising this point, to mostly deaf ears, for the past decade. But now, with the upcoming shortage of labour (referred to in the Prologue), we might hear a wider and louder voice of discussion. For the large part, the women interviewed in this book are only able to work full time because they can *afford* full-time childcare, either in their own home or provided by a day nursery or childminder. They consider themselves privileged in that they earn well and can afford to subsidise their child or children's care.

Should they not be offered a tax concession for this employment they offer?

I raised this question with a friend, who, as yet childless, failed to see the point. So I brought up the image of a typical single woman about to have her first child. (Single – because most people assume a married woman would either stay home or that it would be her husband's responsibility to pay for the childcare.) Until the moment she gives birth, this single woman has been earning a decent living. She is not highly paid but is working her way up through publishing beginning as a secretary, hoping to develop her career to become an editor. On a secretary's pay, how is she hoping to afford childcare? Even a full-time childminder would run expensive on one modest salary.

What is this woman to do? Give up work altogether? If she does drop out, she will then fall dependent on the state, living on Income Support until such time, at least, as her child begins school. Isn't that ridiculous? She wants to remain in work. She hopes to build up her career. She is prepared to juggle her time, her loyalty to child and job. But, if she cannot afford the full-time childcare, she will be given no alternative but to drop out of the workforce and live off the state.

Wouldn't a simple tax deduction for childcare solve the problem? Or more workplace nurseries? Or subsidised childminders' fees, for single mothers?

Even if there was a workplace nursery available for her use, as the Workplace Nurseries Campaign points out, a high-flying manager given a Rolls-Royce as a company car and even free petrol would pay less tax on the perk than this same junior secretary putting her child into a nursery subsidised by her employer.

Increasingly, however, it is now being recognised that attitudes to childcare and the importance of women workers has to undergo a major change. A skilled woman who cannot return to work is a wasted investment.

In recent months, the Employment Secretary, Norman Fowler, has repeatedly urged employers to beware of what is now being called the *demographic timebomb*. In a recent report, 'Young People and the Labour Market – A Challenge for the 1990s', they have forecast that the numbers of 16–24-year-olds will drop by 1.2 million, before 1995; there will be a 23 per cent drop in school-leavers between the ages of 16 and 19. By contrast, there will be an estimated 90,000 mothers, aged between 25 and 44, who could return to work by that same year – if provision was made to help them in that process.

The significance for employers will be in finding ways of *retaining and retraining staff* to meet labour shortages. The most significant growth area of the labour market will be *women* workers, many of whom will be returning to work after having children and wishing to combine a satisfactory work and family life.

Yet, a recent European Commission report, 'Childcare and Equality of Opportunity', shows that Britain's record on childcare is one of the worst in the Community. The report found, for example, that the UK has publicly funded services for less than 2 per cent of children under 3, and for less than 1 per cent of children at primary school, compared with 44 and 20 per cent respectively in Denmark which is top of the league.

The UK is also the only state that provides no full statutory maternity leave (with only 54 per cent of pregnant women eligible) and no parental leave at all.

Uniquely, the UK has low employment among mothers and high unemployment among mothers and fathers. The UK is also the only state where employment protection in the area of maternity has been reduced in the last decade.

Some employers – among the leaders are banks and other financial institutions – are leading the way in recognising the need to retain women workers by providing better childcare provision.

The Midland Bank, for example, is setting up three thirty-five place in-house nurseries in Sheffield, Crawley and Beckenham, at a cost of about £35 per child per week; they are already planning to extend the network if successful before the end of the three-year pilot scheme, with other nurseries in Jersey and Reading. The cost of setting up a nursery is not cheap, but it will far outweigh the danger of losing their employees who leave when they become mothers. All the major banks are likely to offer similar provision. Already they have generous career break schemes, for up to five years for potential managers – now being extended to men and women below management levels – without loss of status or salary levels on return.

The European Commission's report concludes that the principal aim of the Childcare network

> is a Europe where the work and responsibility involved in childcare is properly valued and more equally distributed; where parents can reconcile family responsibilities and employment ... in a way that is satisfying and does not involve disadvantage and inequality; and where children get the advantage of a range of positive and enhancing experiences at home, in childcare services and society at large. These aims concern both equality and quality of life.

Here is an example of one company's attempts to improve the situation. A publishing house, which admittedly does not pay competitive salaries to its largely female workforce, is one of several firms that have brought in a system of allowances for pre-school children (ranging from £10 to £35 per week per child), without lowering the parent's salary to reduce the perk. These workers are recognised as being on low wages; a childcare allowance can help them cope with the cost of staying at work. This is the sort of beneficial arrangement, in cooperation with unions, employers and employees, which may be copied by other companies. The committee meets on a regular basis, not to negotiate, because they all believe in the scheme, but to try to improve it. The committee decides on the amount of money to be awarded. They have also run a two-week play scheme during the summer holidays, near one of their sites.

CHILDCARE SCHEME RULES

1 The scheme will be administered by a committee consisting of a representative from MSF, NUJ, SOGAT and a representative from the Personnel department. The decisions of the Committee will be binding.

2 The criteria for eligibility will be as follows:

—Employee (parent) earning less than £11,580 p.a. (basic salary) – full entitlement.

—Employees (parent) earning between £11,580 and £15,317 p.a. (basic salary) – 50% of full entitlement; (single parent families in this category will be eligible to the full entitlement).

—Employees earning more than £15,317 p.a. (basic salary) will not be eligible to join the scheme.

Where both parents are employed by the Company, the lower of the two salaries will be used as the criteria for eligibility.

An employee's eligibility will be based on his/her salary as at 31 December. During the course of the following year, should an individual receive an incremental payment, retrospective pay award or any other monetary increase, no change will be made to their entitlement.

Part-time employees will receive a pro-rata payment.

All applications should be made to the Committee Secretary, care of the Personnel department.

The payment, payable monthly, will be made to eligible male and female employees who have a child or children of pre-school age until the child/children (youngest child where there is more than one) commences primary school

Note: one payment will be made for a first child under school age. A second child under school age will qualify for half of the first payment. (Additional children will not qualify.)

3 Employees will be eligible to join the scheme on 1 January following completion of six months' permanent service. The six months' permanent service includes a probationary period where applicable. It should be noted that temporary employment will not count towards this service qualification.

4 Eligibility to receive the payment commences when the child is three months old or, if the employee or partner is on

parental leave, when in-company payments cease, whichever is the later.

5 Applications *must* be submitted no later than 31 October.

6 The Committee will meet not less than four times each year to consider all aspects of the scheme's operation.

7 In the fourth quarter of each year, the Committee will assess the overall financial standing of the fund and determine the level of individual payments for the following twelve months, commencing 1 January. The Committee reserves the right to make recommendations to management for an increase in the per capita sum.

8 Management reserves the right to reassess the scheme at any time. In such circumstances, consultation between management and unions will take place, after which appropriate notice may be given for any changes to the scheme.

The structure and management of the Committee will be as follows:

One elected representative from MSF, NUJ, SOGAT.

One management appointee from the Personnel department.

In the event of the Committee being undecided on any matters relating to the operation of the scheme, a vote will be taken.

In addition to the above representatives, a member of the Finance department will attend all meetings in a non-voting capacity to advise on financial matters.

A Committee Secretary (non-voting) will also be appointed from within the staff of the Personnel department.

'Women returners' is becoming a new buzzword or phrase, as employers, teachers and counsellors grapple with some of the problems inherent in encouraging women to get back into the full-time workforce. One company that has been running retraining courses for women, helping them aim their sights high rather than low – gearing them up for new careers in management – is called Dow-Stoker Training Associates, the brainchild of a very forceful young woman (working mother herself), Linda Stoker.

Dow-Stoker are putting into action a National Women Returners Programme, which is being operated in conjunction with many of our leading companies. Recruiting the hidden workforce, says Linda, is indeed going to be a powerful new challenge for the 1990s.

Their career advisers offer guidance on where women should look for employment. The trainers are mostly women returners themselves who have all faced their own personal barriers in getting jobs. They also offer a counselling service to deal with the problems faced by women: perceived difficulties in managing work and family; help in managing a changing relationship with their partners; those women who are still suffering the effects of divorce; and lack of self-confidence. For example, they point out: 'Eighty per cent of women returning to work do not apply in the first instance to a well-known "household name" employer, due to lack of confidence.'

For further information on Women in Management, Wider Opportunities for Women Returners to Work, and the Business Enterprise Programme for Small Businesses, contact Dow-Stoker Training Associates, The Mill, Stortford Road, Hatfield Heath, Herts CM22 7DL (0279 730056).

CONTACTS IN THE CHILDCARE CAMPAIGN

Great Britain

National Childcare Campaign
Wesley House
70 Great Queen Street
London WC2B 5AX

Workplace Nurseries Campaign
Room 205, Southbank House
Black Prince Road
London SE1 7SJ

Equal Opportunities Commission
Overseas House
Quay Street
Manchester M3 3HN

Gingerbread Association for One Parent Families
35 Wellington Street
London WC2

National Childminding Association
204/206 High Street
Bromley
Kent BR1 1PP

National Campaign for Nursery Education
33 Hugh Street
London SW1V 1QJ

National Out of School Alliance
Oxford House
Derbyshire Street
Bethnal Green Road
London E2

National Childbirth Trust
9 Queensborough Terrace
London W2 3TB

Maternity Alliance
59–61 Camden High Street
London NW1 7JL

Working Mothers' Association
23 Webbs Road
London SW11 6RU

NETWORKS FOR WOMEN AT WORK

Association of Women in Public Relations
27 Great James Street
London WC1N 3ES

Association of Women Solicitors
Law Society's Hall
113 Chancery Lane
London WC2

British Association of Women Executives
303 Preston Road
Harrow
Middlesex

British Federation of University Women
Crosby Hall
Cheyne Walk
London SW3 5BA

British Association of Women Entrepreneurs
8 Eyre Court
London NW8 9TT

Career Development Centre for Women
97 Mallard Place
Twickenham
Middlesex

Fawcett Society
46 Harleyford Road
London SE11 5AY

Federation of Business and Professional Women
23 Andsell Street
London W8 5BN

Medical Women's Federation
Tavistock House North
Tavistock Square
London WC1H 9HX

National Association of Women Pharmacists
Pharmaceutical Society of Great Britain
1 Lambeth High Street
London SE1 7JN

National Childbirth Trust
9 Queensborough Terrace
London W2 3TB

National Council of Women
34 Lower Sloane Street
London SW1W 8BP

National Organisation of Women's Management Education
12a Westbere Road
London NW2

National Women's Register
245 Warwick Road
Solihull
West Midlands B92 7AH

Network
25 Park Road
London NW1 6XN

Women in Civil Service
Room 373, Dept of Industry
Ashdown House
123 Victoria Street
London SW1

Women in Computing
c/o Micro Sister
Wesley House, Wild Court
London WC2

Women in Electronics
c/o 34a Gledstone Road
London E5

Women in Engineering Society
25 Foubert's Place
London W1V 2AL

Women in Enterprise
26 Bond Street
Wakefield WF1 2QP

Women in Management
66 Marryat Road
Wimbledon
London SW19 5BN

Women into Management (NW)
85 Abbey Road, Astley
Manchester M29 7WN

Women in Publishing
c/o Brookmount House
62–65 Chandos Place
London WC2N 4NW

Women Returners' Network
Hillcroft College
South Bank, Surbiton
Surrey K6 6DF

Women in Telecom
STE House
Room 212/213 Bath House
52 Holborn Viaduct
London EC1A 2ET

Working Mothers' Association
23 Webbs Road
London SW11 6RU

Australia

Australian Federation of Business
and Professional Women Inc.
NSW Division
GPO Box 1136
Sydney 2001
Telephone: 267 5222

Campaign of Action for Equal Pay
PO Box A222
Sydney South 2000
Telephone: 281 29000

Children's Services Switchboard
66 Albion Street
Surry Hills 2010
Telephone: 212 4144
(Covers the State, any children's services
0–5 and information for
parents and carers.)

Jobs for Women Action Committee
PO Box 1930
Wollongong 2500
Telephone: 042 96 6441
          042 74 6233
          (02) 810 7409

National Association of Community-
based Children's Services
405–411 Sussex Street
Sydney 2000
Telephone: 212 4600
(Advocacy group for the development of
community-based children's services.)

National Consultative and
Advisory Council for Family
Day Care
c/o Warringah Family Day Care
14 The Kingsway
Dee Why 2099
Telephone: 981 2777

NSW Family Day Care
Association
c/o Warringah Family Day Care
14 The Kingsway
Dee Why 2099
Telephone: 981 2727
(Promoting and supporting Family Day Care
Services in the community.)

Women and Employment
Resource Centre
PO Box A222
Sydney South 2000

Women and Management
PO Box Q19
Queen Victoria Building
Sydney 2000
Telephone: 235 0268

Women in Crisis
Counselling Service
Wayside Chapel, Hughes Street
Kings Cross 2011
Telephone: 358 6577

Women's Directorate Department
of Industrial Relations and
Employment Trades Training
for Women
7th Floor, 1 Oxford Street
Darlinghurst 2010
Telephone: 266 8111

Women's Employment Action
Centre
PO Box A222
Sydney South 2000
Telephone: 219 9746
(Diane Hague)

Women's Employment Adviser
Women's Advisory Unit
Department of Employment, Education and Training
9th Floor
Trans City House
15 Castlereagh Street
Sydney 2000
Telephone: 225 8600

Women's Employment Rights
Campaign
30 Percival Street
Lilyfield 2040
Telephone: 662 2097

Women's Liberation House
Room 303, Floor 3
156 Castlereagh Street
Sydney 2000
Telephone: 267 5670

Women's Resource Centre
23 Sheriff Street
Ashcroft 2168
Telephone: 607 7536

Working Women's Advisory Unit
Labor Council of NSW
2KY Building
20 Wentworth Street
Parramatta 2150
Telephone: 635 1066

BOOKLIST

Brannen, Julia and Peter Moss, *New Mothers at Work* (London: Unwin Paperbacks, 1988, £5.95).

Dix, Carol, *The New Mother Syndrome: Coping with Post-natal Stress and Depression* (London: Unwin Paperbacks, 1987, £5.95).

Having a Baby? Know Your Rights (USDAW, Women's Dept, Wilmslow Road, Manchester, M14 6IJ. Send an A5 envelope and postage).

Hewlett, Sylvia A., *A Lesser Life: The Myth of Women's Liberation in America* (London: Michael Joseph, 1987.)

Lew, Irvina S., *You Can't Do It All: Advice That Works for Mothers Who Work* (New York: Berkley Books, 1986).

Sanger, Sirgay and John Kelly, *The Woman Who Works, the Parent Who Cares: A Revolutionary Programme for Raising Your Child* (New York: Perennial Library, 1988).

Shreve, Anita, *Remaking Motherhood: How Working Mothers Are Shaping Our Children's Future* (New York: Fawcett, 1988).

Stechert, Kathryn, *The Credibility Gap: How to Understand the Men in Your Business Life – And Win by Your Own Rules* (Wellingborough, Northants: Thorsons, 1988).

Velmans, Marianne and Sarah Litvinoff, *Working Mother* (London: Corgi, 1987, £5.95).

The Working Mothers' Handbook: A Practical Guide to the Alternatives in Childcare (Working Mothers' Association, 23 Webbs Road, London, SW11 6RU, £1.75. A very popular guide to the intricacies of finding good childcare. Write for the booklet, membership and information on regional groups).